THE SUPREMACY CLAUSE

The Laws of Man that Reveal the Love of God

THE SUPREMACY CLAUSE

The Laws of Man that Reveal the Love of God

David Myers

FITLY SPOKEN

PRESS

This book is a publication of

Fitly Spoken Press
1021 Emerson Dr NE
Palm Bay, FL 32907

http://www.fitlyspokenpress.com

Telephone Orders: 321-723-2030
Email Orders: orders@fitlyspokenpress.com

Unless otherwise noted, Scriptures cited are taken from the King James Version.

ISBN: 978-0-9836707-0-4

Printed and bound in the United States of America

Dedicated to my wife, Aimee, and my children: Gregory, Luke and Sophia.

You continue to inspire me every day.

Table of Contents

❖

Foreword

❖

Law is a profound and powerful creation of God. When understood and used properly, law is designed to protect life, not destroy it. Law brings order out of chaos and is the bulwark between liberty and tyranny.

The Declaration of Independence is one of the most significant documents in American history. What was a death warrant for Founders became the birth certificate for America and the liberty that would spread throughout the world.

Thomas Jefferson was the primary drafter of the Declaration, but the ideas contained therein were not unique to Jefferson. He referred to the Declaration as "the reflection of the American mind." The concepts, and even many of the phrases contained in the Declaration, reflected the American mind because they were commonly held beliefs. The Declaration of Rights drafted by George Mason in Virginia, shortly before the Declaration, contained some of the same phrases and ideas. In fact, each aspect of the Declaration had been preached repeatedly by ministers of the Gospel.

While Jefferson may have added an elegant writing style to the Declaration of Independence, the substance was commonly shared among the Colonists. The Declaration begins with the common understanding that the Creator endowed each person with unalienable rights. These rights do not come from government or from the consent of the governed. They originate with God and are infused in each person because God created each one in His image. Government is not the author of these rights. If government is not the author, then government cannot take away these rights.

Government therefore has a singular duty according to the Founders – namely, government must protect the rights that originate from the

Creator. Thus, civil servants – ministers of justice – have a delegated duty to protect what God created.

The Declaration lists a few of the primary rights God infused in each human being. These include life, liberty and the pursuit of happiness. The right to life is the right of all rights. Without life there is no liberty, and without liberty there can be no pursuit of happiness. A government that does not protect life will soon take your liberty, and when liberty is restricted, the pursuit of happiness vanishes. The right to own property means nothing to a corpse.

The revolutionary ideas contained in the Declaration of Independence gave birth to the most powerful, inventive, and free country in the world.

The fundamental premises of the American Revolution and the French Revolution stand as polar opposites. The former spoke of life, liberty and the pursuit of happiness. The latter spoke of liberty, fraternity, and equality. Life was absent from the French Revolution. Thus, the symbol of the French Revolution was the guillotine.

The American Revolution begins with God. The French Revolution begins with man and human reason. In the American Revolution, the place of government begins with the recognition that there is a God who created human beings and infused them with unalienable rights, and thus government's declared duty is to protect these rights.

In the French Revolution, there is government and only government. There is no God. Thus, rights come by the grace of the government. Government can bestow rights and government can take them away. This includes life. Those who dissent – well, they lose their head! That's why the guillotine became the symbol of the French Revolution.

The word "fraternity" encapsulated the French idea that rights come from the group. If the group decides your life is not worth saving, then your life is not worth saving. Since there was no higher authority than the group, the group was the supreme authority. There was no higher law to which earthly law must conform. Whatever the state said was the law, no matter how arbitrary the rule may have been.

Where did the American Revolutionaries get their ideas? They are expressed in the Declaration of Independence, but, as we said, the Declaration was a "reflection of the American mind." While the Founders read the Classics and read from the works of Montesquieu, John Locke, Blackstone, and others, the most commonly cited source by far was the Bible. In fact, the reason America became the most literate nation in the world was precisely because people were taught to

FOREWORD

read so they could read the Bible. The first compulsory education law in America was in the Colony of Massachusetts. It was called "The Old Deluder Satan Act." It was so named because Satan is a deceiver, and the best way to not be deceived is to read and understand the Scriptures. Thus, education was required to teach people how to read.

The Bible teaches that God created Heaven and Earth. He created each person in His image. He is the Author of life. God establishes governments. He sets up magistrates who have a fiduciary duty to the people to administer justice. Thus, there is a higher law.

St. Augustine wrote that earthly laws must conform to higher law. Blackstone confirmed that if an earthly law does not conform to the higher law, then it is no law at all. Blackstone was the source of law for anyone who became a lawyer during the Founding Era.

In his "Letter from the Birmingham Jail," Martin Luther King, Jr. relied on higher law to defend why he obeyed some laws but not others. He wrote that laws which did not conform to God's higher law are no law at all and should not be obeyed.

If we are to have liberty, we must know the source of liberty. The source of liberty is not government. It is God. Government has a limited and prescribed duty – to protect God-given liberty. Liberty begins with life. Without life there is no liberty and without liberty there is no pursuit of happiness.

History is a good teacher. If we ignore history, we are doomed to repeat its mistakes. The history of the American and French Revolutions is illustrative of the two different philosophical foundations for law and government. One works while the other does not. One protects life while the other weighs life on a cost-benefit scale. One gives birth to liberty while the other devolves into tyranny.

Ideas have consequences. Today there are those who want us to forget our history. It is a powerful history indeed. Those who oppose liberty dislike the history of America. They either want us to forget it or to remake it. At the root of this effort lies the battle over worldviews. At the center of this battle is the place and existence of God. Without God, there is no freedom.

—Mat Staver
Director of the Liberty Center for Law and Policy
Dean and Professor at Liberty University Law School
Founder of Liberty Counsel
Leading Constitutional Litigator

Acknowledgments

❖

A famous author once said, "No man is an island." The Bible also states this principle in different words. Suffice it to say that no book is written without a supporting cast. A team of willing and able participants are needed to achieve victory in most struggles of life. Writing a book is a journey and an adventure but it is not accomplished alone.

I would like to express my appreciation to my parents. My mother, who completed her doctorate degree summa cum laude as a senior citizen, instilled in me a hunger for the euphoria of a completed task. My father always encouraged me to pursue my dreams and made those dreams a possibility by his sacrifice while I attended law school both at home and abroad.

My editor, Denise Johnson, who painstakingly edited the manuscript time and time again to make sure it made sense to more than just the author. Her careful eye and watchful guidance was an invaluable source of strength.

My wife, Aimee and my children were kind enough to allow me to rob valuable time from them so I could hide away and write. They are all a gift from God and I treasure them. I thank them for understanding and supporting me to complete this book. I could not have done it without them.

I thank Mat and Anita Staver for their lives of commitment in defending religious liberties in America. Their selfless energy and expertise makes every Christian in America a little safer. Thank you for giving me the opportunity to work alongside of you, and for allowing me to see, firsthand, the joys and challenges of "standing in the gap."

The friends and members of First Pentecostal Church in Palm Bay, Florida where I have the privilege of pastoring, are the greatest people in the world. A special thanks to my friend and fellow minister, Brian Krause for helping me publish this book.

I can't imagine life without the love and guidance of Jesus Christ. I am so glad I was introduced to you at a young age, and I hope I will always be able to lift you up with my words and my actions. You are the joy in the journey. You are the beginning and the end and everything in between. Thanks for your friendship and for your anointing.

David

About the Author

❖

David Myers is Senior Pastor of the First Pentecostal Church in Palm Bay, Florida, and has been involved in numerous ministries over the past three decades. These ministries include youth, evangelism, leadership training, staff development, capital stewardship and overseas missions. David has visited ninety-five countries; preaching, teaching, and building churches.

David began his post-secondary education by graduating with honors from Apostolic Bible Institute. Afterward, David graduated Summa Cum Laude with a degree in Systematic Theology from Southeastern University. Feeling the call of God to continue his education in the field of law, David graduated Cum Laude with a Juris Doctorate degree from Barry University School of Law.

While attending law school, David studied at Oxford University in Oxford, England. He also studied at Trinity College in Dublin, Ireland under U.S. Supreme Court Justice, Antonin Scalia, and at McGill College in Montreal, Canada under the late U. S. Supreme Court Chief Justice, William Rehnquist.

After graduating from law school, David worked at Liberty Counsel with Mat and Anita Staver. Liberty Counsel is an international non-profit litigation, education, and policy organization dedicated to advancing religious freedom, the sanctity of life, and the family. David co-hosted *Law and Justice*, a national television program with Mat Staver and *Faith and Freedom*, a national radio program.

David and his wife, Aimee, are blessed with identical twin sons, Gregory and Luke, and a beautiful daughter, Sophia.

Introduction

❖

The inexhaustible study of God's nature is fascinating. It seems clear that the more we learn about the nature of God, the stronger our relationship is *with* God.

I was raised in a pastor's home and made aware of the value of the Word of God at a young age. Studying the Word of God and the nature of God in seminary school established more than a duty, but also a desire for exploring more about God. A license to learn was birthed.

Building on the foundation of scripture, something came alive for me while studying in law school. Juxtaposing the laws of God and the laws of man, I began to realize that God has a legal nature. He chooses to operate from a legal structure.

God makes the rules, but His nature will not allow Him to violate His own laws. Those self-imposed laws governed His interactions with man. Understanding those laws, allows one to understand why and how God works in any given situation.

Early case law in American Jurisprudence established the fact that the U.S. Constitution was the supreme law of the land and the United State Supreme Court were the interpreters of the Constitution. This became known as the Supremacy Clause. The federal law is supreme to the state law. Certainly there are numerous twists and turns to this legal precedent, yet it remains a time honored principle in our courts.

Not only has God made His Word supreme to His own actions, every law of nature and man is also subordinate to this same supreme Word. The supremacy of God's law is revealed by man's law and the legal nature of God.

Notwithstanding the fact that any study or legal structure will ever allow us to get a complete grasp on God, we can learn more about Him and grow closer to Him through the study of His legal nature. The more we learn of Him, the more we understand His actions or inactions in our lives.

At first glance, it may seem contrary to popular opinion to emphasize the legal nature of God. Most of our attention as 21st Century Christians is on the unmerited favor of God. This emphasis is on the New Testament and the unconditional love of God, yet even the New Testament is a covenant agreement. A contract.

The more we understand of the legal nature of God, the more convinced we become of His love and His favor.

The more we understand of the legal nature of God, the more convinced we become of His love and His favor. The mercy of God and the requirements of God are not mutually exclusive, just as the New Testament and the Old Testament are not mutually exclusive. Each is made stronger by the ties that bind them and the references that intertwine them.

The commandments of the Old Testament and the promises of the New Testament support each other and shout to us from the pages of ancient scripture that God is a law maker, a law giver and a law abider. The laws of man are based on the laws of God, and the laws of God are forever settled in heaven.

Open your heart and mind to the nature of God. Your purpose in life will be strengthened and your passion for God will burn brighter as we unwrap *The Supremacy Clause*.

THE CONSTITUTION
The Infallible Word of God

❖

In my first year of law school, my favorite class was Constitutional Law. I was amazed to learn that many people are very passionate about their views of how the Constitution should be interpreted. During one of our classes, there was a very lively discussion concerning the different ways to interpret the Constitution. One of my minister friends joined the class that day, and we were enjoying the debate.

Not long into the discussion, a fellow student behind us began to address the students with a spirited proclamation on how the Constitution was a living, breathing document. He spoke with such conviction and passion on how the Constitution was alive and growing. He exclaimed that the Constitution is adjusting to the needs of our society. In my mind I visualized the Constitution running around the class with little arms and legs.

After he finished, I turned around and put a dollar bill on his desk. Fully aware that the class knew I was a minister, I said "Where I come from, if someone gives a speech that is passionate, we take up an offering!" After everyone finished laughing, I reached for my dollar, but he refused to give it back. The dollar was a small consolation for losing the impact of his argument.

The Constitution is the backbone of American Jurisprudence. It is often considered the "bible" of legal studies, so all legal authority flows from understanding and interpreting the Constitution of the United States.

I suppose if ten people were in a room, there would be ten different opinions of how the Constitution should be interpreted, but there are two basic schools of thought. The first is called legislative interpretation or modern interpretation. These type of judges or interpreters are called Loose Constructionists. This is the interpretation that my fellow student was addressing in his passionate speech. Loose Constructionists believe that the Constitution was written so that it can adapt to modern norms.

Loose Constructionists favor a liberal interpretation of the Constitution. They hold that the authors of the Constitution did not intend to preserve an unchanging society, but instead meant for the Constitution to adapt as the needs of the nation changed. This school of thought suggests that the court should be free to clarify the vague language of statutes and to interpret rules for practical application.

In a Loose Constructionist interpretation, the Supreme Court considers the constitutionality of important issues in a society that is much different than it was when the Constitution was written. The difficulty is that no one is quite sure where to draw the line and original intent is thrown out the window.

The second school of thought on Constitutional interpretation is called Strict Construction or an interpretation by adherence to the literal meaning of the words used. Strict Construction of a statute (or the Constitution) means simply that it must be confined to such subjects or applications as are obviously within its terms or purposes. (Barron's Law Dictionary, Third Edition)

In legal circles, Strict Construction is often referred to as Originalism or Textualism. It is important to remember that term. Judges that employ this type of interpretation are often called conservative judges. One such judge on the United States Supreme Court that is a big advocate for this type of Constitutional interpretation is the Honorable Antonin Scalia.

In the summer of 1998, I was granted the opportunity to study under Justice Scalia in Dublin, Ireland. One evening during a social gathering some of the students were questioning his position of being a Strict Constructionist. They asked him, "How can you say if it is not enumerated in the Constitution in its original form that you cannot use the elastic nature of the Constitution to apply legal principles?"

Justice Scalia, who was never without a thoughtful and entertaining answer, gave this response. He mentioned that he had a large family and that he believed strongly in educating them without the interference of the state. He said that if a case came before him on the bench that would declare that the Constitution gives an unequivocal right for parents to raise and educate their children without the interference of the state, he could not rule in favor because the Constitution does not enumerate that right even though he believes it strongly.

"However, if the State came to take my children, I would sit on my porch and exercise my second amendment rights by daring them to take my children," Justice Scalia emphatically stated. The second amendment of the U.S. Constitution states that citizens of the United States have a right to bear arms. While it was a little humorous and unusual to think of a Supreme Court judge exercising his second amendment rights, the judge had made his point.

Justice Scalia was saying there are enough guarantees within the enumerated rights of the Constitution that it is not necessary or accurate to invent new ones when societal norms dictate change. He had further illustrated his point by using an example of a subject that he felt passionate about. In other words, even if you feel strongly about the subject matter, you don't violate your principles to gain a favorable outcome. A favorable outcome at the expense of Constitutional manipulation is not only a slippery slope it is judicial malpractice.

This same philosophy is often used in interpreting the Bible. Many modern theologians want to manipulate scripture to fit the desired outcome. The Bible was never intended to conform to our desires or whims. It is our actions that must conform to the Word of God.

In Galatians 1:6-9, Paul the Apostle writes to the church of Galatia with these words of admonishment, "*I marvel that ye are so soon removed from him that called you into the grace of Christ unto another gospel: Which is not another; but there be some that trouble you, and would pervert the gospel of Christ. But though we, or an angel from heaven, preach any other gospel unto you than that which we have preached unto you, let him be accursed. As we said before, so say I now again, If any man preach any other gospel unto you than that ye have received, let him be accursed.*"

Paul was saying in certain terms that we should not be removed from the original message. This interpretation of scripture is a contextual interpretation or strict interpretation. The interpretation of the Constitution and the interpretation of Scripture are both in agreement for the need of contextual compliance.

CHAPTER ONE
Strict Interpretation

❖

In I Kings 13, there is an interesting story about a man from Judah. The man's name is not given; the Bible only says that he was a man of God. This man from Judah went to Bethel and prophesied against King Jeroboam and the practices of the wayward priests. At that time, Israel was under a king that was not a Strict Constructionist, who had abandoned the Word of God and was governing his own way.

When King Jeroboam heard about this prophet from Judah that was speaking against him, he stretched forth his hand to take him by force and the king's hand withered up. Not only that, but the altar split in two just as the man had prophesied. The king had a change of attitude at this point and asked that the man pray for his hand to be restored. The prophet prayed, King Jeroboam's hand was restored, and the king invited the man to come to the palace.

However, this unnamed man refused to go to the king's house because the Lord had told him to not go in and eat or drink, but to return home a different way. So, the unknown man of God from Judah started home a separate direction. Meanwhile, an old man who lived in Bethel and was also a prophet, howbeit a less than honorable one, heard about it and went with his sons to find this man before he returned to Judah. They found the prophet under an oak tree no doubt resting from his journey.

The old man and his sons invited the prophet to come back to their house for food and drink and once again the prophet said he could not because of God's instructions. The old man said, "I am a prophet too and an angel told me to bring you back." The old man had lied. However, the prophet from Judah went with them to their house and as they were eating, the Word of the Lord came to the old man and he told the prophet, because you did not obey the voice of God as He originally spoke to you, you will not make it home alive.

No doubt, this prophet was ready to leave when he heard this message. Perhaps he was wondering why he did not stick to his original plan. Sure enough, he was attacked and killed by a lion before he made it back to Judah. The moral of this story beyond illustrating the need to stick with the original message is that even if someone claims "God told them" or "an angel told them" to do something, if it is against what the Lord has declared through His Word, don't believe it.

The United States Supreme Court made a decision in 1973 in a famous case called *Roe v Wade*, 410 U.S. 113 (1973), that abortion was legal in America under certain guidelines. They arrived at this decision by basing in on a right of privacy. The only problem is that the Constitution never says that there is a right of privacy. It may sound good, but it is not enumerated in the Constitution. Millions of babies have died by this loose interpretation of the Constitution.

The Bible says in Proverbs 16:25, "*There is a way that seemeth right unto a man*, but *the end thereof are the ways of death.*" When we replace the written text with our own judgment, we run the risk of doing more than just interpreting incorrectly, we also run the risk of losing our soul. In a time when many wonder about the correct interpretation of scripture, we can have an assurance that the contextual or original interpretation of scripture will lead us to truth.

If we interpret scripture from an original textual view-point, we do not have to wake up every morn-ing and wonder what we believe.

The interpretation of scripture in light of modern cultural norms necessitates that we constantly change the interpretation because society constantly changes. If we interpret scripture from an original textual viewpoint, we do not have to wake up every morning and wonder what we believe.

Everything about the nature of God is settled. The Bible says "*His Word is forever settled in Heaven.*" God's Word is settled. His nature is settled. His creation is settled. If we as humans evolved, why are we not still evolving? Humans have looked the same for thousands of years. It appears that God goes with the original. The truth is that God created us in His image and it is settled.

James 1:17-18 confirms God's settled nature by stating: "*Every good gift and every perfect gift is from above, and cometh down from the Father of lights, with whom is no variableness, neither shadow of turning. Of his own will begat he us with the word of truth, that we should be a kind of firstfruits of his creatures.*"

It would stand to reason that morality is settled. Morality does not change based on who the president is or the latest popular movie. Morality is settled because it is based on a document that is settled, the Bible. Laws must be based on a moral code and our moral code comes from the Word of God. Once the anchor begins to move everything shifts.

From the scriptures it is clear that we must stick with the textual or original interpretation of the Word to stay on tract. The prophet from Judah was originally given the word to not turn in and eat or drink. The secondary word that he received from the other prophet was false. He changed his convictions and got off tract.

When Paul instructed the church to beware of others coming and teaching a different doctrine, he referred to their original teaching. If you begin to interpret the scriptures in light of modern norms you get away from the truth because now the text becomes subject to an interpretation that mixes in man's motive and man's imagination.

CHAPTER TWO
Original Intent

❖

Upon my graduation from law school, I had the wonderful experience of working with Mathew (Mat) Staver, the founder of Liberty Counsel, a religious civil liberties education and legal defense organization. One of the most enjoyable and yet eye-opening experiences I had at Liberty Counsel was when our Ten Commandments case (from McCreary County, Kentucky) was granted audience with the United States Supreme Court. Mat Staver gave the oral arguments before the Supreme Court. My wife and I were able to attend with our Liberty Counsel team. The case was *McCreary County v. ACLU*, 545 U.S. 844 (2005).

The issue concerned whether or not McCreary County could hang the Ten Commandments (often called the Decalogue) in a courthouse in Whitley City, Kentucky, if the document was surrounded with other historical documents like the Bill of Rights and U.S. Constitution. Our case was combined with a similar case out of Texas called *Van Orden v. Perry*, 545 U.S. 677 (2005) where a Decalogue monument was on the state grounds in Austin, Texas. These cases were examined to determine if they violated the establishment clause of the first amendment.

The establishment clause is derived from the first amendment of the U.S. Constitution that states in part, "Congress shall make no law respecting the establishment of religion nor prohibiting the free exercise thereof...." The restriction on Congress that has now been expanded to every form of local government comes from the first part of the amendment to limit the state from endorsing a state religion. The free exercise clause comes from the second part and limits what the government can do to restrict the free exercise of a person's faith. The tension between the two clauses is what courts struggle with in religious first amendment cases.

During the oral arguments, Mat made a case for the fact that the Ten Commandments are more than just a religious document, it is also a legal and a moral document. At this point, Supreme Court Justice Ruth Bader Ginsburg interrupted Mat's presentation and asked him if he had ever even read the first five commandments. He recognized the question was a rhetorical question and waited for the judge to finish her statement. She continued by saying emphatically with a tremendous amount of disdain; "Not only are they religious in nature, but they express exclusive worship." I started to shout *Hallelujah* and then realized I was at the Supreme Court. It seemed interesting to me that what repulsed her made me want to rejoice.

Mat then mentioned that the Supreme Court had included in its marble carvings in the frieze above the court the image of Moses with the Ten Commandments. Justice Ginsburg stated that the tables only had roman numerals from one to ten on the tablets so many people think that it could be the first ten amendments to the Constitution. Doesn't it seem odd that Moses would be carrying around the Bill of Rights on a stone tablet?

Our opposing counsel was an attorney for the American Civil Liberties Union (ACLU). Interestingly enough, before being seated on the high court, Justice Ginsberg was an attorney for the ACLU as well. Opposing counsel made a few points with the court by getting the court to focus on an issue that was outside the legal discussion of first amendment jurisprudence. Opposing counsel kept saying that the Decalogue was put up originally to make a religious statement and then the other documents were added to make it pass Constitutional mustard. This would be the equivalent to the team that loses the Super Bowl crying foul because the lights were in their eyes. Nonetheless, time ran out as counsel rebutted the assertion. It proved to be a pivotal issue in the court's curious decision.

On June 27, 2005, the court announced its decision in *McCreary County vs. ACLU*, 545 U.S. 844 (2005). The Supreme Court made a decision not to make a decision. In a 5 to 4 decision, the court stated that the Decalogue could remain on the state grounds in Austin, Texas because it had been there for over 40 years. In the same breath, the Supreme Court ruled against the Kentucky counties that hung up the Ten Commandments in a historical context by the same 5 to 4 margin stating that the counties' "original intent was of a solely religious nature."

Thus, the United States Supreme Court "split the baby" like Solomon suggested in his judgment, and created more chaos than clarity. One county could hang the Ten Commandments up in a courthouse and it is Constitutional, but if the county next door displayed the Ten Commandments, that display could be declared unconstitutional. It would all be based on the courts trying to determine what the intent of the defendant is on a case by case basis.

This decision was roundly criticized by most legal scholars. The average person walking down the hall and seeing the Ten Commandments on the wall has no idea what the original intent was of the person that hung the document. This kind of Ad Hoc justice is both divisive and irresponsible. It shows just how divided the Court is, and the incorrect use of original intent as a legal principle in a Constitutional case.

In more profound and less political decisions concerning the Constitution, judges will often look for the original intent of our founding fathers to better understand the balance between the establishment clause and the free exercise clause. Did the founders mean that there should not be prayer in our schools or that a manger scene should not be allowed on the grounds of the city hall at Christmas? The courts have found a balance by allowing children to pray, but not allowing it to be led by a teacher during school hours, or Jesus can be in a manger scene as long as there are other secular figures present in the scene.

If one was to look at the original intent of the founding fathers alone, only an elementary observation would be needed to gain clarity. In the waning hours of the First Continental Congress as the founders had reached an impasse, Benjamin Franklin stood and said, "And have we forgotten that powerful Friend? Or do we imagine that we no longer need His assistance? I have lived, sir, a long time and the longer I live the more convincing proofs I see of this truth: that God governs in the affairs of men. And if a sparrow cannot fall to the ground without his notice, is it probable that an empire can rise without His aid? We have been assured, sir, in the sacred writings that except the Lord build the house, they labor in vain that build it. I firmly believe this and I also believe that without His concurring aid, we shall succeed in this political building no better than the builders of Babel."

Virtually every one of the Founders of the United States of America saw a vital link between civil religion and civil government.

Virtually every one of the Founders of the United States of America saw a vital link between civil religion and civil government. George Washington's admonitions in his Farewell Speech, September 19,

1796, were characteristic of the general sentiment: "Of all the dispositions and habits which lead to political prosperity, religion and morality are indispensable supports. And let us indulge with caution the supposition that morality can be maintained without religion. Reason and experience both forbid us to expect that national morality can prevail in exclusion of religious principles."

To determine what the intent of the Founders were, courts and attorneys often refer to the Federalist Papers. These are the writings of the Founding Fathers that are not included in the Constitution, but give us insight into their thinking and their intentions. When these papers are read, it is clear that the intent of the Founders was that this nation be built on faith, prayer, and religious freedom. To think that mayors and judges and city council members who have a similar intent will now make them in violation of the same Constitution, is a testament to how far we have moved away from strict interpretation and original intent.

The original intent of our country's Founders is important, but not nearly as important as the intent of our Creator. We know that the original intent of our Creator was to create us in His image. Without sin and without death. The intent was not pain, poverty, shame and despair. The intent was that none would perish. What changed all of this? Sin. This was the risk of a free will, but the real master of the universe had a contingency plan, it's called Salvation. I believe there is great relief when we realize that everything is in the control of the Creator, even things that we do not understand.

There are three directives God set in motion from the foundation of the world that nothing can stop. Not sin, not death, nor the rise and fall of nations can halt God's plan. Let's look into the inspired papers of the Word of God and find out the original intent of our founding Father.

In Ephesians 1: 4-5, the Bible states, *"According as he hath chosen us in him before the foundation of the world, that we should be holy and without blame before him in love: Having predestinated us unto the adoption of children by Jesus Christ to himself, according to the good pleasure of his will."*

A PEOPLE (THE CHURCH)

From the first day, God determined that He was going to have a holy people referred to in scripture as His bride (Jeremiah 33:11, Revelation 21:9). It was not His intent for people to be lost. For people to be unholy or unrighteous. It was never God's intent that people would suffer and hurt. God's original intent was to marry humanity or be legally committed to His people.

The enemy is in the business of trying to convince us that God does not love us and that God is not helping us, but the intent of our maker was that we would be without blame. Sin tries to change this. The enemy tries to convince us that we are losers, but God said before you were even born, I loved you.

Jeremiah 1:5 states, *"Before I formed thee in the belly I knew thee; and before thou camest forth out of the womb I sanctified thee, and I ordained thee a prophet unto the nations."*

Matthew 25:34-35 states, *"Then shall the King say unto them on his right hand, Come, ye blessed of my Father, inherit the kingdom prepared for you from the foundation of the world: For I was hungry, and ye gave me meat: I was thirsty, and ye gave me drink: I was a stranger, and ye took me in."*

A PLACE (HEAVEN)

From the very beginning, God has prepared a place. It's not just a place, it is a palatial place. God did not create hell for humanity. He made heaven for us. When someone prepares a place for us; that makes us feel wanted.

I remember when we use to visit my grandmother at Thanksgiving. There were kids all over the house, and my grandmother did not have enough beds for all of the children, so she made pallets on the floor in front of the fireplace. A Five Star hotel could not have made us feel more loved and welcomed. Is there anything that offers you more hope than your Savior? Is there anything that has more of a future?

The Bible explains that this place called Heaven has walls of jasper, streets of gold, and gates of pearl, but what will make this place so great? A hint is given in John 14, *"I go to prepare a place for you, that where I am, there you may be also."* The fact that we will be with the Lord is the greatest reward of all.

Revelation, chapter 13 verses 8-10 says, *"And all that dwell upon the earth shall worship him, whose names are not written in the book of life of the Lamb slain from the foundation of the world. If any man have an ear, let him hear. He that leadeth into captivity shall go into captivity: he that killeth with the sword must be killed with the sword."*

A PLAN (REDEMPTION)

Before there was sin, there was a way out. I believe one of the biggest lies that the Devil tells us is that we will never change. We are trapped in sin. We cannot get out. We need to remind our enemy that we know the founder, we know the Father and we know what His intent is. God intends for us to be saved. He not only intended for it to happen. He has a *plan*. He has a *path*. He has a *purpose*. God intends for us to make it.

Before there was sin, there was a way out

CHAPTER THREE
The Supremacy Clause

❖

The Supreme Court of the United States is one third of a tripartite system that the American Government is built on. The other two branches are the legislative branch and the executive branch. To many, the judicial branch is the most powerful branch of government in our modern times, but it was not always like that. John Jay, the first Supreme Court Chief Justice, was given the job because no one else wanted it. In early America, the justices had to ride circuit and go from state to state judging cases. This all changed when John Marshall was appointed Chief Justice.

John Marshall, who was a former Secretary of State, was appointed by President John Adams in the eleventh hour of his presidency. John Marshall turned out to be a brilliant choice as he wrote opinions that still shape our judicial system today. Chief Justice Marshall wrote the majority decision in *Marbury v. Madison*, 5 U.S. 137 (1803) that greatly expanded the reach of the judicial branch. Basically, Justice Marshall said that the Constitution was the "supreme law of the land," and it is the job of the United States Supreme Court to interpret it. The brilliant writing of Justice Marshall went unchallenged.

Article VI of the U.S. Constitution says "This Constitution shall be the supreme law of the land and the judges of every state shall be bound thereby, anything in the Constitution or laws of any state to the contrary notwithstanding." In one quick stroke of the pen, *the Supremacy Clause* was born.

In the court system of England, one must go from the Magistrate's Court to the Crown Court, then to the Queen's Bench, and finally to the House of Lords. Over the House of Lords is the European Court of Justice. If England passes a law that is in conflict with the European Court of Justice, the law is null and void. This does not sit well with many in England, but it is the price they must pay to be a part of the European Union. Every judicial system has a supreme law.

The supreme God that we serve has the final say in all matters. There is no higher law and there is no greater power. Hebrews 6:13 states, *"He could swear by none greater, so he sware by himself."* Since God has a supreme status, when the ideas of man conflict with the laws of God, the ideas of man are doomed. When the concepts of false teachings purvey useless information, they

> *The supreme God that we serve has the final say in all matters.*

may flounder and flop around on the canvas of human curiosity for some time, but when they rear their ugly head against God's law they are on a collision course with extinction.

The brilliant theologian and philosopher, Francis Schaeffer, shook the scientific world when he wrote his thesis, *No Final Conflict.* He said in this thesis "the scriptures are unchallenged not only where they touch that which is considered religious, but also where they touch history, science, and the cosmos." He went on to say, "the Bible is not a scientific textbook, its theme and central purpose is to give us what fallen man needs to know between the fall and the second coming of Christ. It does so through two specific revelations and two general revelations. The two specific revelations are the verbalized communication from God to man in the Bible and the revelation of God in Christ. The two general revelations concern the universe and its form and man and his surroundings. When modern science conflicts with these revelations, give it time and the scientific theories will eventually be discarded."

There are those that may put their basis of belief on this earth through new age teachings and some may put their faith in the stars through horoscopes and astrology. The Bible says in Mark 13:31, *"Heaven and earth shall pass away: but my words shall not pass away."* Isaiah 40:8 tells us, *"The grass withereth, the flower fadeth: but the word of our God shall stand for ever."* **Everything bows to the Bible. That is God's Supremacy Clause.**

In the decades of the 1960s and 1970s when Earl Warren was Chief Justice of the United States Supreme Court, the court began to swing radically to the left. The laws in America began to change with liberal justices enjoying a majority. It was during this time that in addition to *Roe v. Wade,* 410 U.S. 113 (1973) and *Engel v. Vitale,* 370 U.S. 421 (1962), the school prayer case, *Miranda v. Arizona,* 384 U. S. 436

(1966), established the famous Miranda rights that are given when a person is arrested.

Eventually, the court began to shift more conservative. This slow shift did not go unnoticed by the court. The remaining liberal justices who were becoming the minority saw the handwriting on the wall and became concerned that the changes in the law that the court had made in the sixties and seventies would be overturned by this more conservative court.

An idea was proposed and set forth in a Harvard Law Review article in 1977 by Justice William Brennan, a remaining liberal Supreme Court Justice. The idea suggested that states could develop strong State Constitutions to protect these individual rights. Justice Brennan proposed different formulas whereby states could insulate themselves from Federal Review. He suggested that State Constitutions could provide more individual rights than the U.S. Constitution, but not less, and if court decisions were based solely on the State Constitution and state cases, then the United States Supreme Court had no authority to review and reverse these state decisions.

This was a clear sign that the Supreme Court wanted the states to get more involved as the court shifted more conservative. But states were having problems implementing this proposal because they were not creative in their State Constitutions. The states would only try to mirror what the U.S. Constitution already had in place. This lock step legislation with the Federal Constitution relinquished independence from federal review. In other words, the supremacy of the United States Supreme Court stood. This small island of adequate independent ground proved to be difficult for individual states to find.

The enemy of our soul cannot create.

The enemy of our soul cannot create. All he can do is copy. He is always trying to copy God's power and God's authority. The difficult notion for Satan is that every time he tries to duplicate what God is doing with a counterfeit, he insures supremacy in the hands of the originator. The Creator. The Supreme God.

When Moses and Aaron were establishing their authority to lead the children of Israel out of Egypt, Aaron threw down his rod on the ground in Pharaoh's court and it became a snake. The sorcerers in the Egyptian court acting as copy cats did the same thing, but the Bible says that the rod of Aaron that had become a snake ate up all of the other snakes. (Exodus 7:12) The Egyptian sorcerers had not only lost the authority battle, they also lost their rods. Let's see if anyone can copy that! That is God's Supremacy Clause in action.

The Bible declares that *"Greater is he that is within you, than he that is in the World."* (1 John 4:4). When our enemy comes around with his bag of tricks, he tries to insulate himself from the judgment of God by convincing us to rely totally on him and forsaking all reliance and dependence on Jesus Christ. If our enemy can, he will try to insulate himself from being overridden by God, because God will not violate our own free will.

In the United States, if we just mention the name of the court or we refer to the court's domain, and If we just consider a federal case or a federal constitutional provision, the Supreme Court has all power and authority to overturn. Likewise, if we just mention the name of Jesus. If we just refer to His greatness. If we just consider His law, watch Jesus step in and overturn the death sentence that Satan has pronounced on us. Jesus is Supreme.

In *Michigan v. Long*, 463 U.S. 421 (1983), Justice Sandra Day O'Connor writing for the majority in the U.S. Supreme Court said if we are not sure and it is not clear if the lower court is relying on the State Constitution or the Federal Constitution, we are going to presume that federal law is applicable. In fact if one does not want us involved, a brief statement in the decision must be composed that states: *"this case rests solely on state law and state cases, and is independent of any federal law."* This ruling from the U.S. Supreme Court gave birth to the Plain Statement Rule.

If we want to keep Jesus out of our life we have to be very clear to denounce his authority in our life. The supremacy of Jesus and His law can find the crevices and cracks in our heart and His power can penetrate even the uncertainty of a sinner. There is a presumption that we are still relying on His grace even when we get off track. Don't disprove that presumption. In the end, the supremacy of God's law will trump even our own will.

In the end, the supremacy of God's law will trump even our own will.

17

CHAPTER FOUR
Prevailing Authority

❖

I grew up hearing the Bible taught by my father who pastored our church. I also grew up hearing my mother say, "Because I said so". This usually followed a question that I had concerning her authority. Now that I have children of my own, I place more value on the chain of command or as the Word says, authority.

When my son, Luke, was five years old, he asked me, "Dad, do you have to answer to God?"

I said, "Yes."

"And mom has to answer to you?" he continued. I nodded cautiously wondering where this conversation was going.

"And we have to answer to mom?" I affirmed.

"Then what are my brother and I over?" he wondered.

Gregory, his identical twin, ever prepared to accommodate, quickly said, "Our toys."

I laughed and Luke was not satisfied. Luke looked at me and said, "I want to be over more than just toys."

I suppose it is in the nature of mankind to want to be the boss. That has gotten us in trouble since the beginning. Many of our laws are meant to curb that ambition and to bring order to a civilized society. According to Barron's Law Dictionary, Third Edition, the word *Constitution* in terms of American law refers to "a written instrument which is the basic source from which government derives its power."

The Constitution is the basic law in which all others must conform, but in citing case law for a written brief or a legal memorandum there are prior cases that are controlling and others that are suggestive. Controlling authority comes from a higher court or higher authority while suggestive decisions come from sister courts or courts that are at a similar level of authority. When appealing to a higher court, this prior case law is not a controlling authority and does not have to be followed. One is binding and the other is discretionary.

If the laws of God can be better understood by the examples and illustrations of the laws of man, then our faith in God's laws as well as His principles and precepts will be strengthened. Psalms 119:11 says, "Thy word have I hid in mine heart, that I might not sin against thee."

The Church derives its power from the Word of God. It is interesting to see how many churches and denominations have left and abandoned the position that the Word of God is without error. Once we begin to forsake the authority of the scriptures, then it is a foregone conclusion that we will also begin to mitigate our power.

Many formal religions are at a crisis point because they have meetings with no anointing and with no authority. They seek to return to the principles that they were founded upon to recover their power. The same principle is true in our individual lives. If we forsake the Word of God as the constitution or the sole source of authority in our lives, then we will begin to lose power or authority in our life. We cannot dictate the choices in our life, and we begin to only react to the circumstances in our life. We become spiritually and emotionally reactive rather than proactive.

If we forsake the Word of God as the constitution or the sole source of authority in our lives, then we will begin to lose power or authority in our life.

The Word Gives Us Authority

The absolute grip on the inerrant and infallible Word of God is the greatest source of strength afforded mankind. Once we have His Word and the established authority in our own life, then we have the necessary foundation for the construction of a life built on principles that have authority.

When I look around at the world that we live in, and I see the decisions and choices that people are making, it seems clear that we have a lack of authority in our lives. We respond as slaves to our feelings and emotions rather than as masters deciding and choosing based on godly principles.

One of the interesting aspects to raising a child is to teach them that what they want to do is not and should not be the supreme law in their heart. One of my sons explained to me recently upon my inquiry as to why he did something that he was told not to do. He said he did it because he "wanted to."

"It doesn't matter if you wanted to do it, you were told not to do it and that is more important than what you want to do," I explained. He seemed to understand, but I see that it is a battle the next time he has to make a decision. This struggle is true with all of humanity.

If we make a decision that the Word of God has greater weight than our own desires in the choices that we make and we follow that guidance, then we have the authority in our lives to make wise choices. Those wise choices give us greater freedom and stability in life. It is the fundamental secret to a successful life.

When Moses was negotiating with Pharaoh about the children of Israel being released from captivity, Pharaoh was struggling with the concept that there was a higher authority than him. It took a series of plagues for him to be convinced. The plague of hail and death had been pronounced and Exodus 9:21 says, *"He that feared the word of the LORD among the servants of Pharaoh made his servants and his cattle flee into the houses: And he that regarded not the word of the LORD left his servants and his cattle in the field."*

Even among the servants of Pharaoh there were people who allowed the Word of God to be a controlling authority in their life and there were those that rejected the Word of God as discretionary. This principle applies to everyone on earth, even those that are not part of God's family.

The Word Gives Us Sustainability

Barron's Law Dictionary, Third Edition, says that the Constitution gives us "a permanence and stability to government." The permanence of man's law pales in comparison to God's law, but nonetheless illustrates the nature of humanity to sustain its environment in a structure of laws.

Deuteronomy 8:1-3 says *"All the commandments which I command thee this day shall ye observe to do, that ye may live, and multiply, and go in and possess the land which the LORD sware unto your fathers. And thou shalt remember all the way which the LORD thy God led thee these forty years in the wilderness, to humble thee, and to prove thee, to know what was in thine heart, whether thou wouldest keep his commandments, or no. And he humbled thee, and suffered thee to hunger, and fed thee with manna, which thou knewest not, neither did thy fathers know; that he might make thee know that man doth not live by bread only, but by every word that proceedeth out of the mouth of the LORD doth man live."*

The key word in that verse is *live*. Day to day. The authority of God's Word gives us a consistency to life. A consistency that stabilizes us and sustains us. Although we are temporarily in this life, God's Word gives us permanence.

One of the more interesting things about our Constitution is how it is still relevant after all of these years. It still applies. It still rules. It is the backbone of our judicial system. It is the backbone of our economy. It is the backbone of the political structure. The Word of God is the backbone of God's judicial nature and God's economy. It is the constitution, so to speak, of all that God does to interact with man and keep order in this universe. God's Word will never be outdated or irrelevant. Life is literally sustained by the Word of God.

The Word of God is the backbone of God's judicial nature and God's economy.

We cannot change the Constitution with a lesser statute. The Constitution is the supreme law of the land and cannot be abrogated even in part by statute (140 Federal Supplement 925, 928). Deuteronomy 4:2 says, *"Ye shall not add unto the word which I command you, neither shall ye diminish ought from it, that ye may keep the commandments of the LORD your God which I command you."* The sustainability of the Word of God is due to the fact that it cannot be changed. We can change, but the Word of God is forever settled in heaven.

The Word Gives Us Protection

"The Constitution is not designed to protect majorities, who can protect themselves, but to preserve and protect the rights of minorities against the arbitrary actions of those in power." (Barron's Law Dictionary, Third Edition)

Authority is not given so one can boss others around. Authority is based on specific skill and knowledge. In trial, attorneys call expert witnesses to speak as an authority on a specific subject. They must establish the witness' expertise before the witness testifies.

The Word of God as the controlling authority in our life protects us. When the man Christ Jesus was weak in his flesh after 40 days of fasting, Satan came to temp Him and to flex his supernatural power. Jesus resisted and overcame Satan by using the Word of God as a protection. To each of Satan's temptations, Jesus said, *"It is written…. It is written….It is written…"* Three times Jesus resisted temptation by referring to the Word of God. The Word protected Him in a weaken state. The Bible says in Matthew 4:11, *"Then the devil leaveth him, and, behold, angels came and ministered unto him."*

In Acts 19:16-20, we see a clear case of authority, *"And the man in whom the evil spirit was leaped on them, and overcame them, and prevailed against them, so that they fled out of that house naked and wounded. And this was known to all the Jews and Greeks also dwelling at Ephesus; and fear fell on them all, and the name of the Lord Jesus was magnified. And many that believed came, and confessed, and shewed their deeds. Many of them also which used curious arts brought their books together, and burned them before all men: and they counted the price of them, and found it fifty thousand pieces of silver. So mightily grew the word of God and prevailed."*

The Word of God prevailed in their lives and in their community because they made it the ruling authority in their life.

CHAPTER FIVE
Standing

❖

It is no small accomplishment to have access to places of importance or value. In a rewards program for frequent guests, many major hotel chains will program one's room key so they have access to the concierge level. In the concierge, one enjoys extra benefits such as sodas or water. Breakfast is available in the morning and hors d'oeuvres in the evening. Newspapers and computer printers are also available. In the few times I had access to the concierge floor; I learned that there is an interesting atmosphere of superiority that exists. New people come in the door and everyone looks at them as if to ask, "Are you sure you are here legally?"

I have been in several situations where I was on the receiving end of a "you don't belong here" glance. Once, President Ronald Reagan came to our hometown to celebrate the city's 100th birthday. He was scheduled to have lunch with 300 of the city's leaders. I was able to talk one of the advance team members into giving my father and I tickets to this special luncheon. I positioned my father and myself very close to the President much to the chagrin of the event organizers. Our aggressive seat posturing and the abundance of secret service agents with bulges under their jackets was disconcerting for my father. My father kept saying, "We are going to get shot!" I am not sure how much he enjoyed the luncheon, looking over his shoulder the entire time and wondering if we were going to be removed at any moment.

Constitutional law has a special word that it uses to describe access. It is called *standing*. One must have *standing* to have access to the courts. A plaintiff, or the person who is bringing the claim against another person, must have a significant stake in the controversy to have standing. The plaintiff must show that he has suffered an "injury in fact." That is, the plaintiff must show that he has himself been injured in some way by the conduct that he complains of. One cannot bring a suit for an injury to someone else, with the exception of minors who do not have individual standing in American courts due to age restrictions.

To have *standing*, **one must not only be the person with the injury, but the injury must be concrete and individuated.** The injury or harm cannot be presumed or the possibility of a future injury. Then, one must satisfy the requirement of bringing a cause of action that is the cause, in fact, of the injury. In other words, one must have a cause of action or claim that is directly related to the injury. One cannot bring a suit for an issue that does not directly relate to the injury.

The Bible tells us in Hebrews 4:16 that we can *"come boldly unto the throne of grace, where we may obtain mercy, and find grace to help in time of need."* God gives us access to the throne room. We are able to come into his presence and to make our petitions known to Him. This access was not always granted. In the Old Testament, only the high priest could come into the throne room or the Holy of Holies. This is where the presence of God was represented with the Ark of the Covenant. Access was limited. Only Moses could go to the top of Mount Sinai when the law was given. In fact if any of the people or even the cattle touched the mountain they would be slain. (Hebrews 12:20)

Beyond just the fact that we are blessed because we are able to enter into His presence, the question that arises is how did we get this access to God's throne room? The writer of Hebrews says that we have this access through Jesus Christ, our High Priest, who was *"tempted in all points like as us yet without sin."* (Hebrews 4:17-18). Consider the access in light of the requirements of Constitutional *standing*. The injury of sin is personal and is to every individual. The Bible says *"we have all sinned and come short of the glory of God."* (Romans 3:23). So, we have met the requirement that we have *standing* through the individuality of the injury.

At the point of Jesus giving up His life, access was granted to every individual.

We are, in fact, injured from sin and Jesus has the answer to that injury. Since we have been injured through sin, the requirement is met that we have an injury in fact. Our request is that we be delivered from sin so the cause of action is directly related to the injury in fact. Our petitions go to the throne room that can actually do something about the injury. Jesus has the authority to give us relief from the injury of sin by the mere fact that he conquered sin. He became the remedy for our injury. That is why we can find help in the time of need. Not only did His blood provide the antidote for sin, but we are also healed by the stripes that were laid to His back. (1 Peter 2:24)

The Bible tells us that when the blood of Jesus was shed on Calvary, that the veil was ripped in two in the tabernacle. (Mark 15:38). This was the veil that separated the Holy of Holies from the rest of the tabernacle and limited access to the presence of God. At the point of Jesus giving up His life, access was granted to every individual. You can go directly to the Lord now. No other man has to take our petition for us. The legal requirements of *standing* were met for each of us to go into the throne room, to go into the heavenly courts of justice, and find the remedy of rest for our soul.

Article 3 section 2 of the Constitution limits federal court jurisdiction to "cases and controversies." The court does not just give an advisory opinion, that is, opinions which just give advice about legislative or executive action when no party is before the court who has suffered specific injury. This Constitutional limitation is meant to limit the time the courts spend on any action that will not offer specific relief.

The Lord is interested in being able to fix us. We do not serve a God who is in the business of just offering advisory opinions. The solutions to life are found in the Word of God. The Bible is not just a collection of stories that will give us a warm, fuzzy feeling. The Word of God gives you a judgment. It declares the issues of life. It is a remedy for everything we face on a daily basis.

We do not serve a God who is in the business of just offering advisory opinions.

If one is just interested in philosophy, then enjoy the Bible on a literary basis. However, if we have a need, if we are hurting, if we desire relief, then the Word of God will direct us into the presence of God, and we will know that we are there legally. We have a right to be in the throne room and no man can take that right from us, even if they give us a funny look, because *standing* was given to us by God.

CHAPTER SIX
The Standard of Review

❖

In the first week of my first year in law school, I had a criminal procedure instructor that frequently referred to accused clients he had defended. In one scenario, I raised my hand and said, "You can't do that!"

He said "Why not?"

I said, "Because there is a constitutional right to…"

He interrupted me with, "Where does the Constitution say that?" I did not know and quickly learned that a constitutional right should be in the Constitution somewhere. The professor had applied a standard of review to my lack of knowledge that is called strict scrutiny. I also learned not to speak until I knew what I was talking about.

Each of my sons is quick to tell me when their brother has done something wrong, but they are slow to tell me when they have committed the same offense. They apply a different standard of review for the same offense based on who the offender is.

There are different standards of review that are used in constitutional law to determine if a governing body has violated an individual's constitutional right. Let's examine the three main ones.

The first standard of review is rational review or weak scrutiny. This standard only requires that the Government show it has a "legitimate" state interest and that the law is "rationally related" to that interest. A very small percentage of laws are struck down when rational review is applied. If the judge decides to apply rational review to the case then the government entity that is defending will win in most cases. It is such a low standard that it is difficult for the plaintiff to show that the governmental entity did not meet this standard. This standard is often used to decide equal protection issues.

The next standard of review is intermediate scrutiny. If this standard is used, then the government must show that the law is "necessary" to achieve a "substantial," or important governmental interest, and that the law is "narrowly tailored" to that interest. This is a real sliding scale, adjusted up and down based on philosophy, composition, and whim. This is the standard of review that is often used in gender discrimination cases.

Strict scrutiny is a standard of review that is used to examine any law or statute that restricts or limits a fundamental right. The legal language is "a significant interference with the exercise of a fundamental right." The Standard for Compliance requires that the governmental body passing the legislation in question bears a heavy burden of justification to show that the law is "necessary" to promote a "compelling" state interest and is being accomplished in the "least drastic and intrusive way". (Barron's Law Dictionary, Third Edition)

Strict scrutiny applies to fundamental rights which the courts have interpreted as the right to vote, to interstate travel, to education, to marriage and procreation, and to content-based free speech. The class of people that face restrictions from governmental statutes based on the classification of race or nationality will often be rewarded with strict scrutiny as the standard of review for their complaint. From a practical standpoint, any statute or law examined under strict scrutiny almost always will fail, so the real battle is to get the courts to examine a statute under a different standard such as intermediate scrutiny or rational review. The question then becomes what standard of review is going to be used to examine the constitutionality of a law or statute by a governmental body. This standard is determined early on and is really the determining factor in most constitutional cases.

The question for most Christians as we apply Biblical principles to the thousands of decisions that we make every day is: What standard of review will we use? If someone takes the name of the Lord in vain in our presence either in person or in media format; how do we react to that? Our reactions are based on how we immediately review that infraction in our spirit.

The real battle is what standard do we use? Do we look at this intrusion as a serious, intermediate or minor offence? Our reactions are based on the immediate judgment that was made and the immediate judgment was based on the immediate classification that we gave the infraction.

Have you ever wondered why similar stories can make you laugh and angry? Recently, I received two different humorous stories in my email. Both were similar in nature, but because of the different standard of review that I immediately used, one upset me and one made me laugh. In principle they may not have been that different, but because in one of the jokes I felt the nature of God was the centerpiece of the humor, and in another the government was the object of ridicule, I classified them differently. The nature of God is vital to my salvation and the government's latest bill is not.

There are certain areas that are non-negotiable with God. There are certain aspects of God's essence that He puts such a high value on and it would serve us well to pay close attention. The following are six areas of God's essence where God applies strict scrutiny.

1. His Presence

In II Samuel 6:3-7, we read that when David was moving the Ark of the Covenant to Jerusalem, the ark started to fall off of the cart. Uzzah, one of the men who walked alongside, put his hand on the ark to steady it. The Bible says that immediately God smote him for his error and Uzzah died. The reason that this punishment was so harsh was because it was the Ark of the Covenant which represented the presence of God.

In Exodus 19:12-13, we read that when Moses went to the top of Mount Sinai, he was instructed that neither the people nor their cattle could touch the mountain. If they did they would die. This may seem overly harsh, but God applies strict scrutiny to things that represent His presence. We should always give reverence to the presence of God. If you are in a church service and the Lord is moving, you may want to pay attention because the Lord is applying strict scrutiny to your actions and reactions to His presence.

2. His Position

The Old Testament law was built around two very important principles denoted in the following two scriptures: *"Hear O Israel, the LORD our God, the LORD is one."* (Deut. 6:4) and *"Thou shalt have no other gods before me."* (Exodus 20:3) These laws that were given to Israel at its inception were based on the position of God. He is alone. There is none beside Him. He is high and lifted up. He does not share His throne. Anything that comes against this fundamental truth is going to be judged by God with strict scrutiny. Settle this truth.

One of the interesting things about strict scrutiny under constitutional law is that laws are often shot down under strict scrutiny because they are too vague. Vagueness is a big factor in killing many statues that would seek to infringe on a fundamental right. Think about this in terms of the vagueness of traditional doctrines that minimize or mitigate the position of God. Vagueness in the identity of God is going to be shot down every time. There is only One God and His name is Jesus.

3. His Place

God does not like it when anyone messes with His house or even the things in His house. He took out Belshazzar and the Babylonian crowd when they started to drink and defile the vessels of the temple in Jerusalem that they had stolen. (Daniel 6) In the New Testament, this was demonstrated again. Jesus went after the money changers in the temple because they were selling pigeon doves and had turned the temple into a flea market. He drove them out with a whip. That is strict scrutiny.

God went after the sons of Eli when they defiled His temple with their sins.

1 Samuel 2:22-25 tells the story, *"Now Eli was very old, and heard all that his sons did unto all Israel; and how they lay with the women that assembled at the door of the tabernacle of the congregation. And he said unto them, Why do ye such things? For I hear of your evil dealings by all this people. Nay, my sons; for it is no good report that I hear: ye make the LORD'S people to transgress. If one man sin against another, the judge shall judge him: but if a man sin against the LORD, who shall intreat for him? Notwithstanding they hearkened not unto the voice of their father, because the LORD would slay them."* There is an interesting dichotomy given here that is worth exploring. It is evident that God's place and His people are very precious to Him.

It is evident that God's place and His people are very precious to Him.

4. His People

When Balaam, the Old Testament prophet, tried to curse the children of Israel for money, He was unable to do so. When Balaam opened his mouth, only blessings came out. (Numbers 22) God looks after His people.

David said in Psalms 37:25, "*I have been young, and now am old; yet have I not seen the righteous forsaken, nor his seed begging bread.*" It is our nature of self preservation that causes us to become stressed when we can't pay bills or worried beyond measure when we can't provide adequately for the ones we love, but we must trust the Word of God that reassures us that God takes the provision of His people seriously. If he has to send a raven in a desert to deliver food, he will do it because of the standard of review that He applies to our needs.

5. His Priesthood

God will not let us dishonor His anointed and get away with it. He smote the siblings of Moses for questioning Moses' authority and accusing Moses of making himself to be something he was not. God smote the siblings with leprosy. This is one reason that David would not kill King Saul. (I Samuel 24) David had been instructed by his father, Jesse to respect God-given leadership. Jesse may have told David: *The king may not always be right, but it is not our job to try and fix it.*

I know this is an unpopular subject, but it is a Biblical principle that needs to be addressed. If one of God's men is doing wrong, God will take care of it. Let God do His job. If there are spiritual abuses, God will reveal it in time. You should be cautious about putting yourself in the position of being an accuser of the priesthood, because God uses strict scrutiny on this kind of behavior.

6. His Person

The Bible says "*He came unto His own and His own received Him not.*" (John 1:11) Many of those that were fellow Galileans with Jesus, struggled with accepting the person of God in the form of Jesus. This was a vital fundamental truth that many missed and it cost them dearly.

The person of God is critical to understanding the plan of God. God enshrines this principle by hallowing the name of God. The person of God is not separate from the name of God. The person is Jesus. He is the fleshly manifestation of God. When Satan came against the person of God, he was defeated. When man came against the person of God, he was defeated.

Sins of the Father

We are in an era where the person of God is either praise or pillaged based on how we treat the name. If we take the name of God in vain, then we are disrespecting the person of God. Not a good thing to do. If we praise the name of God, then there is favor of God, because He applies strict scrutiny to the person of God and the things that represent the person of God. *Sins of the father* **are sins that directly relate to rejecting the nature and sovereignty of God.** Sins that blaspheme His authority. Sins that ridicule His word. Sins that reject His sovereignty.

Sins of the Flesh

Sins of the flesh **have a natural consequence built in even before God judges them. In this area, there is more of an intermediate scrutiny that God uses to examine the offence.** These kinds of sins are addictions of the flesh. If one uses illegal drugs, the body judges perhaps even before God does. If one abuses alcohol, the body judges rapidly…usually by the next morning.

We sometimes think of these types of sins as the worst sins, but that is not how God looks at it. God looks at the heart and sees *sins of the father* as more of a heart issue than *sins of the flesh*. It does not mean that the sin is less; it just means that God has more to work with when a person is struggling with *sins of the flesh* rather than *sins of the father*. I know I run the risk of losing the principle with the example, but consider Adam and Eve. They did not get thrown out of the garden for running around naked. They were thrown out for disobedience. Sins of the father.

God looks at the heart and sees sins of the father as more of a heart issue than sins of the flesh.

My young sons are often fascinated with noises as most boys are, especially noises that their bodies can make. I am trying to teach them that this is impolite. This is important, but being disrespectful to their mother or disobedient to an authority figure is more egregious and examined under strict scrutiny.

One day at pre-school one of my sons, (I won't tell you which one in case he reads this book) was in the bathroom for a long while. The teacher told us later, he began to sing loudly saying, "I love the Lord. He is wonderful. Jesus loves me." He was singing at the top of his lungs. The teacher knocked on the door and checked to make sure he was okay. Out of the corner of her eye, the teacher noticed that my son was sitting on the commode without a stitch of clothes on. No socks, no shoes, no shirt, no pants, nothing. He told the teacher he would be out in a minute and went back to singing.

I would rather my son learn that he does not need to totally undress to go to the bathroom, but singing on the commode at the top of his lungs about how much he loves Jesus in a school with his peers made me smile because it revealed his heart.

Jesus had more of an issue with the attitudes of the Pharisees than he did with the woman caught in adultery. I don't say this to encourage sins of the flesh, but only to encourage one that God can deliver us from the sins of the flesh. We don't want to disqualify ourselves from the plan of God because of the sins of the flesh in our past. We must go forward, sin no more and keep our heart right. God removed Saul from the throne because of the sins of the father; his disobedience. However, God kept working with David even after David committed sins of the flesh.

In Romans, the writer records the heart of God with these words, "*Jacob have I loved, but Esau have I hated.*" Why? Does God love some and not others? **He loves everyone, but *sins of the father* are examined under strict scrutiny and *sins of the flesh* under intermediate scrutiny.** Esau was ambivalent about the things of God. Jacob was hungry for the things of God even though he struggled with his flesh.

Sins of Forgiveness

Sins of forgiveness are sins we commit against each other. *Sins of the father* are sins committed against God. *Sins of the flesh* are sins committed against one's body. *Sins of forgiveness* are examined under rational review. This review requires only a legitimate governmental interest and the law rationally related to that interest.

God said He would forgive each of us with the same spoon that we forgive others. God's forgiveness of us will be in proportion to our forgiveness of others. (Matthew 7:2) If we have a hard time forgiving others, it doesn't mean that God hates us, it just means that our mercy from God is going to be limited. It is directly related to how much mercy we show to others. That is a lot of motivation for each of us to be merciful to others.

The mercy of God is undeniable. Every sin is capable of being sanitized and eliminated with the blood of Jesus. No sin is more acceptable because each sin serves to separate us from a holy God. If I sin against my God, my own body or my neighbor, I have an advocate or a mediator in the person of Christ Jesus (I Timothy 2:5.) The victories of the person of God are made available to us through repentance. The person of God through a heavenly judicial system can grant clemency to the gravest of crimes.

CHAPTER SEVEN
Life

❖

The book, *Endurance*, by Alfred Lansing chronicles an expedition in 1914 to the bottom of the world. The ship on which the crew sailed, also called *Endurance*, eventually became locked in a sea of ice that crushed and sank their vessel. Men stood watching nearby on a floe as their only link with home slid out of sight.

In preparation for the journey, Captain Earnest Shackleton placed the following ad in the local newspapers of London, England. It read "Men wanted for hazardous duty. Small wages. Bitter cold. Long months of complete darkness, constant danger. Safe return doubtful. Honor and recognition in case of success."

The response was phenomenal. More than 5,000 men applied, of which only 27 were accepted. One stowaway also managed to make the journey. One would have to ask, why were so many men willing to risk everything to be a part of this perilous adventure?

Working hand-in-hand with the Constitution, the Declaration of Independence was written to guarantee individual rights. On July 4, 1776 the Declaration of Independence of the United States of America was adopted by the Second Continental Congress. The second section states, *"We hold these truths to be self-evident that all men are created equal, that they are endowed by their Creator with certain unalienable rights, that among these are life, liberty and the pursuit of happiness."*

The phrase can also be found in Chapter III, Article 13 of the 1947 Constitution of Japan, and in President Ho Chi Minh's 1945 Declaration of Independence of the Democratic Republic of Vietnam. These unalienable rights may be guaranteed by our Constitution and recognized by other democracies, but they are given by our Creator.

Jesus said it this way in John 10:10, *"I am come that they might have life, and that they might have it more abundantly."* Life is more than just having a pulse and breathing air. This cornerstone of our democratic government is often lost in the legalese of court decisions and political gamesmanship. Like most things, you have to go back to the Bible to get clarity. It makes sense and even the Declaration of Independence acknowledges that life is endowed from the Creator.

In John 12:25-26, Jesus said, *"He that loveth his life shall lose it; and he that hateth his life in this world shall keep it unto life eternal. If any man serve me, let him follow me; and where I am, there shall also my servant be: if any man serve me, him will my Father honor."*

This verse may sound like suicide, but it isn't. The Lord is giving us some profound insight about how to have abundant life. The key here is the word love and it is the first of three principles that the Bible gives us to get back to the unalienable right of life.

1. Service

It you love your life, the amenities, the pleasures, the comforts, then you lose the joy of life. The joy of the simple things. The joy of helping a neighbor. The joy of spending a day with your family at the park. The joy of picking up someone for church. If you refrain from the pleasures of this world, from the self gratification, from the constant pursuit of fleshly fulfillment, you gain something much more valuable. There is a peace, a joy, a sense of destiny and value that the world cannot explain.

Galatians 5:13 says, *"For, brethren, ye have been called unto liberty; only use not liberty for an occasion to the flesh, but by love serve one another."*

Service is a secret that people are tapping into. Volunteering is at an all time high. As a nation we are volunteering by the millions. Why are people doing this? Because it is rewarding to serve others. Not monetary compensation, but a sense of purpose. Knowing we have made a difference in someone's life is the greatest reward we can receive. Our profession is what we are paid to do, but our calling is what we are *made* to do.

Each year I take a group of men overseas to build a church in a third-world country. I never cease to be amazed how men are affected by these mission trips. These men volunteer their time and pay their own expenses in addition to giving up vacation time. Many of them are saving for the

Life is serving

next trip as soon as they return. Many have expressed to me how they are changed by this experience for life. These men have learned what the Bible teaches. Life is serving.

2. Sacrifice

The ability to commit yourself to a cause that is bigger than yourself brings a spark to the soul even though your body must make a sacrifice.

Matthew 6:24-26 says, "*No man can serve two masters: for either he will hate the one, and love the other; or else he will hold to the one, and despise the other. Ye cannot serve God and mammon. Therefore I say unto you, Take no thought for your life, what ye shall eat, or what ye shall drink; nor yet for your body, what ye shall put on. Is not the* **life more** *than meat, and the body than raiment? Behold the fowls of the air: for they sow not, neither do they reap, nor gather into barns; yet your heavenly Father feedeth them. Are ye not much better than they?*"

The men that answered the ad to explore on the ship *Endurance* were not affected negatively by the warning of "bitter cold, small wages, months of darkness and a small chance of survival." In fact they were energized by the challenge to the point that 5,000 men wanted the assignment. This is an example of how the sacrifice is not a deterrent, but rather a stimulant. The ability to commit yourself to a cause that is bigger than yourself brings a spark to the soul even though your body must make a sacrifice. Life is more than the absence of death; it is defeating the doldrums of a mere existence with purpose and sacrifice.

3. Submission

The Bible tells us in I Peter that our liberty comes from submission. When we live in humility, we live an abundant life. Modern philosophy from a narcissistic world tries to tell us that you will be happy when you are in charge. Our Bible tells us you will be free when you submit one to another.

In fact the Bible says that there are three areas that we need to submit: To each other (Ephesians 5:21), to those that have the rule over us (Hebrews 13:17) and to God (James 4:7). Submission may go against the grain of our flesh, but it is the secret to really living.

CHAPTER EIGHT
Liberty

❖

Patrick Henry, speaking on March 23, 1775 at St. John's Church in Richmond, Virginia is credited with swinging the balance in convincing the Virginia House of Burgess to pass a resolution delivering the Virginia troops to the Revolutionary War. He spoke with conviction to rally the fledgling group of patriots.

"They tell us sir that we are weak; unable to cope with so formidable an adversary. But when shall we be stronger? Will it be the next week, or the next year? Will it be when we are totally disarmed, and when a British guard shall be stationed in every house? Shall we gather strength by irresolution and inaction? Shall we acquire the means of effectual resistance by lying supinely on our backs and hugging the delusive phantom of hope, until our enemies shall have bound us hand and foot?"

The struggle for liberty is the thirst of humanity. To have liberty is to have an unfettered soul. Liberty is oxygen to our inner most being. Liberty is what makes our nature thrive; our spirit to soar. Liberty is interlaced with hope and the manifest expression of our will. Liberty is freedom and freedom is not free. It must be valuable because men and women shed their blood to ensure its place in our nation's history. However, beyond that our *spiritual* freedom required blood to be shed on Calvary.

Liberty is what makes our nature thrive; our spirit to soar.

The Declaration of Independence states that we have an unalienable right to liberty. These words were meant for the King of England to read and to understand that this spirited group of colonists was getting their authority from a higher power. Our laws are based on this concept of liberty. We enshrine it. We interpret it in judicial decisions. But do we really have liberty or are we only "hugging the phantom of hope?"

The Apostle Paul wrote in II Corinthians 3:17, "*Where the Spirit of the Lord is there is liberty.*" If liberty is attached to the core of our being and it is, and if liberty is the foundation of our country and it is, then it would only stand to reason that what gave us our foundation came from the Spirit of the Lord. Spiritual liberty is desired as much as physical liberty.

As a young boy, my concept of liberty was when the school bell rang and classes were dismissed. We were free to play ball and visit our friends. The greatest threat to our freedom was the idea that parents and school officials could set rules and laws requiring us to be in school. At the age of 12, we knew what real liberty was and it became obvious to us that there was a massive conspiracy from authority figures to restrict our freedom. The paradox of such a perspective is this: The rules and laws that we thought were captivity, in reality, were our ticket to freedom.

In my first year of law school, our criminal procedure professor told us American jurisprudence is based on the underlying principle: "It is better for 100 guilty men to go free, than one innocent man to go to prison." This would insure us of the liberty intended by the signers of the Declaration of Independence, the professor explained. I took issue with that interpretation. I countered that this type of thinking actually restricts our freedom. When people are fearful about walking down the streets of their neighborhood after dark, have we really preserved liberty?

This freedom fueled the engines of a young nation driven by dreams of democracy and steered by the determination of hard work.

History demonstrates that as a culture continues to embrace instant gratification at the expense of future freedom, society begins to unravel morally. The fire hydrant of freedom that propelled America in its infancy was agreement that the preservation of principles comes at the expense of personal prosperity. This freedom fueled the engines of a young nation driven by dreams of democracy and steered by the determination of hard work.

When the concept of liberty becomes redefined as the pursuit of pleasure, the underlying tenet loses strength and the fire hydrant is reduced to a trickle. "Pay now and play later" is exchanged for "Play now and pay later."

In II Corinthians 3:5, Paul states, *"Not that we are sufficient of ourselves to think any thing as of ourselves; but our sufficiency is of God."* True liberty begins with understanding our limitations as humans. That is one reason that early in our nation's history we incorporated God and His will into our decisions and our foundation as a nation. We recognized our limitations. We based our laws on the recognition of human limitation and our freedoms on the recognition of moral restraint.

In his book, *Slouching Towards Gomorrah*, Robert Bork explains, "Real freedom is the space in between the walls. It is healthy to discuss how far apart the walls should be, but it is cultural suicide to have all space and no walls." The walls are rules and laws that keep freedom flowing. Rules and laws do not threaten our freedom. They protect our freedom. Restricting my behavior now will ensure me of freedoms and choices for the rest of my life. A society that believes in handing the next generation more than a higher Dow Jones average, will embrace the safety of personal disciplines and the consequences for the lack thereof.

In the Bible, the Old Testament is often criticized for all of its rules and laws. Many Christians will exclaim with a sigh of relief, "We no longer live under the law!" The notion that God's law brings freedom often produces a chuckle. Some believe that the law puts us in bondage. Nothing could be further from the truth. The law stands as a wall protecting our freedoms and protecting our choices.

The law stands as a wall protecting our freedoms and protecting our choices.

The Bible tells us in Deuteronomy 6:24 why God gave us the moral law: *" to fear the Lord our God, **for our good always**, that he might preserve us alive, as it is at this day."* The fire hydrant of freedom that flows from such a holy book is shrouded in laws and commandments. It becomes a trickle when modern day society embraces gratification and pleasure without the protection of sacrifice and discipline.

What is freedom? Is it the ability to do as we please? Is it the release of 10,000 red, white and blue balloons at a political convention? Is freedom defined as the license to pursue personal fulfillment or is it just the smell of hot dogs and the sight of fireworks on the fourth of July?

Patrick Henry continued his speech, "Sir, we are not weak if we make a proper use of those means which the God of nature hath placed in our power. The millions of people, armed in the holy cause of liberty, and in such a country as that which we possess, are invincible by any force which our enemy can send against us. Besides, sir, we shall not fight our battles alone. There is a just God who presides over the destinies of nations, and who will raise up friends to fight our battles for us."

He then concluded with words that still ring in our ears: "The next gale that sweeps from the north will bring to our ears the clash of resounding arms! Our brethren are already in the field! Why stand we here idle? What is it that gentlemen wish? What would they have? Is life so dear, or peace so sweet, as to be purchased at the price of chains and slavery? Forbid it, Almighty God! I know not what course others may take; but as for me, give me liberty or give me death!"

The cradle of liberty was self sacrifice rather than self fulfillment.

The cradle of liberty was self sacrifice rather than self fulfillment, but this was not new with our founding fathers.

The opportunity of choice is a trickle of freedom, the ability to make the right choice is the definition of real freedom. More than 2000 years ago, Jesus had a choice. One choice would give Him immediate, but limited freedom. The other choice would bring ultimate freedom to many, but cost Him His life. The right choice at Calvary ensured that the fountain of freedom would never run dry for Christians that embrace the law.

CHAPTER NINE
The Pursuit of Happiness

❖

The story is told of a woman who was at work when she received a phone call that her small daughter was very sick with a fever. She left her work and stopped by the pharmacy to get some medication. She got back to her car and found that she had locked her keys in the car. The woman looked around and found an old rusty coat hanger that had been left on the ground, possibly by someone else who at some time had locked their keys in their car. She looked at the hanger and said, "I don't know how to use this." She bowed her head and asked God to send her help. Within five minutes a beat up old motorcycle pulled up, with a dirty, greasy, bearded man who was wearing an old biker skull rag on his head. The woman thought, "This is what you sent to help me?" However, she was desperate, so she was thankful.

The man got off of his cycle and asked if he could help. She said, "Yes, my daughter is very sick. I stopped to get her some medication, and I locked my keys in my car. I must get home to her. Please, can you use this hanger to unlock my car? He said, "Sure." He walked over to the car, and in less than a minute the car was opened. She hugged the man and through her tears she said, "Thank you so much! You are a very nice man." The man replied, "Lady, I am not a nice man. I just got out of prison today. I was in prison for car theft and have only been out for about an hour." The woman hugged the man again and with sobbing tears cried out loud, "Oh, thank you God! You even sent me a professional!"

Happiness is not limited to just positive circumstances; we can find a way to be happy in any circumstance. **What exactly did the founding fathers of America mean when they described us as having unalienable rights to pursue happiness?**

The phrase "pursuit of happiness" appeared in the 1967 U.S. Supreme Court case, *Loving v. Virginia*, 388 U.S. 1 (1967). Chief Justice Warren wrote: "The freedom to marry has long been recognized as one of the vital personal rights essential to the orderly pursuit of happiness by free men." An earlier judicial opinion, in *Butchers' Union Co. v. Crescent City Co.*, 111 U.S. 746 (1883), had, however, considered Jefferson's phrase in the Declaration of Independence to refer to one's economic vocation of choice rather than the more ephemeral search for emotional fulfillment, even though one may be predicated on the other.

U.S. Supreme Court Associate Justice Stephen Johnson Field, in his concurring opinion to Associate Justice Samuel Freeman Miller's opinion, wrote: "Among these inalienable rights, as proclaimed in that great document, is the right of men to pursue their happiness, by which is meant the right to pursue lawful business or vocation, in any manner not inconsistent with the equal rights of others, which may increase their prosperity or develop their faculties, so as to give to them their highest enjoyment."

The first amendment is meant to protect individuals from government intrusion. Therefore, it provides liberty to individuals and restraint on the government. This liberty is part and parcel to the concept that we should be unshackled to pursue happiness.

In its entirety, the First Amendment says: "Congress shall make no law respecting the establishment of religion, or prohibiting the free exercise thereof, or abridging the freedom of speech, or of the press, or the right of the people peacefully to assemble, and to petition the government for a redress of grievances."

The laws of our land have developed to protect individuals from government intrusion and unlawful intrusion from each other. This would allow individuals to pursue happiness. The only problem is learning how to protect ourselves from ourselves. Often times we are our own worst enemy when it comes to happiness or the pursuit thereof. The answer may be in the freedom of speech.

A freedom of speech case requires the following constitutional analysis. First you must identify four parts: the parties, the forum, the restriction, and the test.

The Parties

There must be a governmental party and a private party. The first amendment restricts the government, so if both adversarial parties are private, there is no first amendment case.

The Forum

There are three forums:

1. A traditional public forum (a street, a sidewalk or a park)
2. A limited public forum (a public school used by private groups)
3. A nonpublic forum (not intentionally opened for expressive activity, airport)

Restrictions or Restraints

1. A content neutral restraint (for example a parade permit that is required of everyone)
2. A content based restraint (permits political speech, but not religious speech)
3. A viewpoint restraint (allows speech, but only from Democratic not Republican view)
4. A prior restraint (requires a speaker to gain permission prior to speaking)

The Test

Each forum has four tests depending on the restriction involved. Once the applicable test is determined, that test should be utilized in order to determine if there is a First Amendment violation of our freedom of speech.

As fascinating as that might be, no sarcasm intended, it pales in comparison to another law that is higher and another document that is more powerful....God's Law and God's Word. Before Thomas Jefferson, John Adams or George Washington, there was a giver of freedom to pursue true happiness. Consider these types of free speech that are not guaranteed by the Constitution alone, but more importantly the Creator:

1. Freedom to Worship *(The expression of the soul.)*

When Jesus rode triumphantly into Jerusalem near the end of His earthly ministry, the Bible tells us that children in the streets came out and worshipped Him. They waved palm branches and sang songs. The religious leaders rebuked Jesus for allowing these children to worship Him like this. They demanded that He stop the people from worshipping Him. Jesus said *"If these should hold their peace the very stones would immediately cry out."* (Luke 19:40) This is an insight given to the nature of man. We were created to express ourselves. We were designed by the Creator to worship. This is a freedom that comes from God.

You can't restrict worship. You can't stop the soul from leaping. From the very beginning of time, God put it in our nature to want an atmosphere of adulation. To find a place where the soul can erupt in the presence of God. The lions in the Roman Colosseum could not stop it. The iron curtain in the former Soviet Union could not stop it. The bamboo curtain in China is not stopping it. The heavy-handed laws and fear tactics of Islam will not stop it.

Regardless of race, religion, language, color or creed, the soul will find a way to worship. Paul and Silas demonstrated in Acts 16 that even physical affliction cannot restrict worship. The restriction is removed because a freedom of speech petition has been filed in heaven, and the giver of life and liberty determines that the restriction is unmerited in this forum of the heart that wants to worship.

Remove the restriction. Loose the vocal chords. Praise comes forth. The pursuit of happiness is only fulfilled when we use our voice to express worship to our Creator. If we choose to use this freedom of the soul to express criticism and damnation, then we lose the God-given right to pursue happiness through worship.

2. Freedom to Witness *(The declaration of the soul.)*

Whether or not we realize it, our soul wants to declare something.

In Acts 4:19-21, Peter and John said to the religious leaders, *"Whether it be right in the sight of God to hearken unto you more than unto God, judge ye. For we cannot but speak the things which we have seen and heard. So when they had further threatened them, they let them go, finding nothing how they might punish them, because of the people: for all men glorified God for that which was done."*

How can you stop the soul from confessing faith? If my mouth will not work, then my life will shout it from the rooftops. If my speech is impeded, then my actions will declare it. Whether or not we realize it, our soul wants to declare something. That's why we can't buy it off with the accumulation of wealth. We can't get our soul drunk on pleasure and chill its voice. We can't drug our soul on immorality and indecently. We can't confuse it with false doctrine. Our soul still has a message that it is shouting from the crevices of our inner most being.

3. **Freedom to Believe** *(The salvation of the soul.)*

It is not a mystery to me that the evidence of salvation is linked to speaking. *"For with the heart man believeth unto righteousness; and with the mouth confession is made unto salvation."* (Romans 10:10)

When 120 people gathered in the upper room began to receive the Holy Ghost in Acts 2, it spilled out into the streets and people came and gathered together to hear what this was all about. The crowd on the street heard a declaration that was evidence of an unfettered soul. The Apostle Peter begin to preach unto them and he quoted David who they all knew and loved as a great King of Israel.

Acts 2:26-29 records Peter's words, *"Therefore did my heart rejoice, and my tongue was glad; moreover also my flesh shall rest in hope: Because thou wilt not leave my soul in hell, neither wilt thou suffer thine Holy One to see corruption. Thou hast made known to me the ways of life; thou shalt make me full of joy with thy countenance. Men and brethren, let me freely speak unto you of the patriarch David, that he is both dead and buried, and his sepulchre is with us unto this day."*

Peter began to tell them that David is dead, but Jesus rose again. He then violated every public speaking rule of alienating your audience by saying, *"You crucified him, but God hath declared Him to be Lord."* (Acts 2:36). The three thousand people that were added to the church that day were simply the overflow of a freedom to believe. All of this came from the impetus of believing and speaking.

The heart can say yes in any environment and in any circumstance. The pursuit of happiness came from God. Laws were developed to keep the government and others from unduly burdening that right. We as individuals must use that right and protect that right by disciplining the tongue to declare the things of God.

THE CONTRACT
The Covenants Between God and Man

❖

Early on, my twin sons introduced me to the concept of contract law. The simple language of "you said so" was all they needed to bind me. I could not always remember what I had said, and that certainly did not help my case.

They were clever enough to use guilt and desire to their advantage in holding my feet to the fire about something I had "suggested." My guilt in not giving them something that they wanted or taking them somewhere that I had mentioned combined with my desire to make them happy and give them every opportunity in life, made their simple arguments quite compelling.

They did not know the concepts of detrimental reliance, offer and acceptance, bargain for exchange or any other formal contract language. This lack of knowledge did not stop them from being tough negotiators. Contract law is used every day in ways that we may not recognize, but especially in our relationship with God.

The Lord gave us two contracts in scripture that we call testaments or covenants. They are clearly stated in the title of the two divisions of our Bible; the Old Testament and the New Testament. While we may not look at them as contracts, they are in purpose and function.

Barron's Law Dictionary, Third Edition, defines contract as "a promise or set of promises, for breach of which the law gives a remedy, or the performance of which the law in some way recognizes as a duty." The essentials of a valid contract are: parties competent to contract, a proper subject matter, consideration, mutuality of agreement and mutuality of obligation. Understanding the basis of contract law gives greater insight and appreciation into our relationship with God.

CHAPTER TEN
Mutual Obligation

❖

The first example of contract that we see between God and humanity is with Adam and Eve in the Garden of Eden. God gave humanity a beautiful gift...the garden. He clearly laid out the responsibilities and restrictions that went with the garden. The restrictions had consequences just as the law has remedy for breach of contract. One young girl in Sunday School raised her hand and asked her teacher, "I went to a wedding with my parents yesterday and the people getting married kissed right in the church, is that okay?" This young girl thought she had seen a breach of contract even while the contract was being established.

> *Biblical scriptures repeatedly confirm that God honors the law. He plays by the rules.*

It is easy to look back at the first of all human contracts and question why God would put a tree in the garden that could not be touched and fruit on the tree that could not be eaten. Some say, "God is trying to trip them up by putting something in the garden that looks good and tastes good, but cannot be partaken of." **We want the benefits without the boundaries, but the truth is that every promise has a duty.**

The responsibilities were clear. Genesis 15: 2 says, *"And the LORD God took the man, and put him into the Garden of Eden to dress it and to keep it."* A contract is not valid without a **"performance of which the law in some way recognizes as a duty."**

Our relationship with God is enhanced when we realize that we have a duty. We have a responsibility in the mutual agreement. It is more fun to think of God as a spiritual Santa Claus that will gives gifts without responsibilities, but it is not sound contractual law.

Biblical scriptures repeatedly confirm that God honors the law. He plays by the rules. He binds himself to a set of laws that He has established. This notion may seem one sided or unilateral, but it becomes bilateral when we see how God binds himself.

God will not expect performance on your part without binding Himself to a mutual duty. In the case of the Garden of Eden, He performed by giving the Garden of Eden, and then sustaining it with the River of Life (Genesis 2:10). In other words, He cared for the Garden before He ever required Adam to care for the Garden.

The contracting parties were put on notice in Genesis 2:17, *"In the day you eat thereof, you shall surely die."* The consequence for breaching the contract was clear. This fulfills the requirement of contract law that states, "for breach of which, the law gives a remedy." A remedy for one party is a consequence for the other.

Humanity often struggles with the notion that our relationship with God obligates us to certain actions. During my early ministry, I remember teaching a Bible Study to a young couple. As we sat together with our Bibles opened on their kitchen table; discussing the creation of humanity, the question was posed to me: "Why does God require us to obey Him?"

Notwithstanding the fact that God is God and we are His creation, contract laws of mutual agreement bind equal parties. The fact that God would contract with us as equal parties is amazing! It shows His love for us and His willingness to subject Himself to the rules of the law.

In the case of *Ray v. William G. Eurice & Brothers, Inc.*, Md. Ct. App., 201 Md. 115, 93 A.2d 272 (1952), the courts found that even though the contractor, William G. Eurice & Brothers, Inc. made a mistake in reading the architect's plans and refused to perform by building the contracted building, it did not release the builder from his responsibility in the contract. The appeals court ruled it did not preclude a meeting of the minds between the parties, thus eliminating an essential element in the formation of the contract.

The mistake was unilateral and not mutual. **Only a mutual mistake can defeat the existence of a contract.** The Bible says in John 5:39 to *"search the scriptures, for in them you think you have eternal life."* There is a duty on our part to know the responsibilities of our side of the agreement with God. Our lack of diligence in reviewing the contract (the Bible) will not release us.

CHAPTER ELEVEN
Consideration

❖

One day when I arrived home from work, my wife said to me, "Your three-year-old sons have been especially active and very difficult today." (Of course, she always uses the phrase, "your sons" when they misbehave.) "Since I am exhausted, I am going to lie down," she continued. "Do you mind putting them to bed?" I said that I would and met the boys in their room.

After talking to them for a few moments, I said, "You must always listen and obey your mother." The boys asked why and I explained, "Because she gave you life. She carried both of you in her stomach for nine months." The boys had a startled expression on their face. They had never heard this before. They asked me what they were doing in mom's stomach. I said, "You guys were just swimming around." They wanted to know if they were wearing their swim trunks, and I informed them that they were not. They wanted to know if they had a night light and I told them that I was pretty sure it was dark. They said, "Dad that is amazing!" I said, "That is why you must always obey your mother, because she brought you into the world." They were chattering between themselves as I prayed with them and turned out the light.

My wife was asleep as I went to bed, so she did not know about this conversation that I had with the boys. The next morning, we awoke with both boys in bed staring at their mom with hands propped up under their chins. My wife opened her eyes realizing that someone was staring at her and said, "What is it?" One of my sons looked at her and asked, "Mom, why did you eat me and my brother?"

A few months later after telling our friends and church members this story, my sons asked me as we rode along in our truck; "Dad, people always like to hear you tell that story, but how did we get in mommy's stomach?" I tried to explain how this is the mystery of life. God gives life and He is an amazing God. We don't always understand how He works. I was proud that I had dodged a bullet when one of the boys staring out the side window said, "Dad, I think you know and you are just not telling us." He was right!

Consideration is something of value that must be a part of any legally binding agreement. Consideration does not necessarily need to be money. Consideration could be something of value in exchange for a performance or a promise of performance. Consideration is what distinguishes a contract from a mere gift.

The Bible is clear that God gives gifts. James 1:17 records that *"Every good gift and every perfect gift is from above."* The giving nature of God should not diminish the fact that many times something of value is required for the promises of God. These conditional promises are a part of the legal nature of God.

Consider the fact that God required Abraham to find ten righteous people in the cities of Sodom and Gomorrah in order to spare these cities from destruction. This requirement was part of a bargain for exchange that Abraham had entered into with God in Genesis chapter eighteen.

II Chronicles 7:14 states *"If my people, which are called by my name, shall humble themselves, and pray, and seek my face, and turn from their wicked ways; then will I hear from heaven, and will forgive their sin, and will heal their land."* This verse shows multiple conditions to the promise of performance.

The blessings of God are not without cost. The promises of God are often contingent on some action. The idea that every blessing of God is a gift without consideration is contrary to scripture and the nature of God. Sacrifice is consideration. Every time we sacrifice something of value in our life to fulfill Biblical principles, we ensure the blessings of God in our life.

When King Solomon sought to build the temple in Israel, God required some things from Solomon to ensure the blessings of God on the project. *"Concerning this house which thou art in building, if thou wilt walk in my statutes, and execute my judgments, and keep all my commandments to walk in them; then will I perform my word with thee, which I spake unto David thy father: And I will dwell among the children of Israel, and will not forsake my people Israel."* (I Kings 6:12-13)

Obedience is sacrifice and sacrifice is consideration.

Obedience is sacrifice and sacrifice is consideration. Often in the Word of God, obedience was required for the blessing. We can understand the value of obedience if we understand that our covenant-oriented God is looking for consideration on our part to make

52

the agreement legally binding. This binding agreement locks out the enemy from stealing what legally and rightfully belongs to us.

Contracts do more than just bind the contracting parties, they also protect the contracting parties from other parties outside of the contract (third parties) making a claim to the legal rights of the contracting parties. This legal instrument protects the binding parties. Third parties cannot come at a later date and try to wiggle their way in without the consent of the contracting parties.

Children are not only a gift from God; they are a part of the contract that gives value to the contracting parties. Children are not only protected from intruders in a spiritual sense, they should also strengthen the marital contract from outside parties. It is the contracting parties (husbands and wives) that determine the strength of that bond. This is why marriage is more than just a piece of paper. Not only was marriage used as an example of God's bond with us in scripture, but it is also the cornerstone of our commitment to the next generation and our commitment to protect the future by protecting the present.

CHAPTER TWELVE

The Identity of the Parties

❖

A group of second grade students were asked to write a letter to God. Some of the letters that they wrote revealed the humorous way that a child's mind works.

Nancy wrote:

"Dear God, It must be hard to love all the people in the world. There are only 4 people in my family and I can never do it."

Mickey wrote:

"Dear God, if you watch me in church on Sunday I will show you my new shoes."

Larry wrote:

"Dear God, maybe Cain and Abel would not kill each other so much if they had their own rooms. It works with my brother."

Joyce wrote:

"Dear God, thank you for the baby brother, but what I asked for was a puppy."

Even for children, mistaken identity is not a foreign concept.

A legally binding contract must clearly state the identity of the parties. Often a government issued form of identification or a notary public is required to establish the identity or the signature of the contracting parties. This is for the purpose of substantiating clear cut identities that will be obligated to the responsibilities of the agreement and enjoy the benefits of the agreement. It also protects the contracting parties from intruders…third parties that do not have the correct identity.

You and I contract with God when we take on the identity of His name. The name of Jesus clearly establishes the identity of the God that we covenant with. Jesus said, *"No man cometh to the Father but by me."* For the enemy of your soul to come along at a later date and try to steal the blessings of God on your life is simply illegal. It cannot happen in the spirit world without your permission or God's permission.

The Bible tells us in Acts 19:13-15 that men not privy to a covenant relationship with God (the sons of Sceva) tired to use the name of Jesus to cast out devils. The power that comes with the name of Jesus is a blessing that is part of a covenant relationship when we take on His name. The sons of Sceva were third parties that tried to enjoy the blessings of contracting parties without the sacrifice of contracting parties. The attempt was illegal in the spirit world and met with disastrous results. (Acts 19:16)

By law I have a certain obligation to the children that carry my name. I am responsible to provide for them and to protect them. It is part of a marital contract that I have with their mother. It's interesting that my obligation to the children of my name continues even if the marital contract is dissolved. Until they take on the name of another or reach the age of majority, I am legally responsible.

If you have coveted together with God through the identity of Christ, added consideration through sacrifice, worship and obedience, then the enemy has no claim to your life or God's blessings on your life.

That is one reason why the enemy had to get permission from God to even touch the possessions of Job. The devil could not touch Job's bank account without God's permission. The enemy could not touch the health of Job without God's permission because he was not part of the covenant or contract. The enemy also could not touch Job's children without God's permission.

You and I cement the blessings of God in the lives of our children when we apply these principles to their lives as well as ours. If children are a heritage of the Lord, and the Bible says that they are, then this covenant agreement will pass down to them.

The disciplines that you instill and the sacrifices that you make in the lives of your children will ensure that God will bless them and will protect that blessing from being robbed. That is why the Psalmist observed in Psalm 37:25, *"I have never seen the righteous forsaken nor his seed begging bread."*

CHAPTER THIRTEEN
Offer and Acceptance

❖

I once heard a story about a doctor that was addressing a large audience in Tampa, Florida. The physician explained that the foods, liquids, and chemicals we ingest into our stomachs are enough to kill us. Red meat is awful. Soft drinks corrode your stomach lining. Chinese food is loaded with MSG. High fat diets can be disastrous, and none of us realize the long-term harm caused by the germs in our drinking water. However, there is one thing that is the most dangerous of all. "Can anyone here tell me what food it is that causes the most grief and suffering for years after eating it?" The doctor questioned. After several seconds of silence, a 75-year-old man in the front row raised his hand, and softly said, "Wedding cake."

Marriage is a great example that any agreement that is formalized must have an offer and an acceptance. An offer without acceptance cannot form a contract and acceptance without an offer cannot form a contract. **When both offer and acceptance are clearly identified, there is an assumption of mutuality of agreement. Mutual agreement is essential in the formation of a contract.**

To constitute a valid offer, there must be language of a promise such as, "I will" or "I do" as opposed to "I may" or "I would like to." There must be a sufficiently definite statement of terms so that an acceptance can be made without the suggestion of new terms. A few years ago, I was rehearsing with a couple that was getting married in a large church wedding. We were practicing the flow of the vows when the groom nervously said, "I think so." I quickly realized we needed more practice before the big day.

The Bible makes it clear that God offers salvation through covenant agreement to all humanity. In John 7:37, Jesus stood and cried, saying *"If any man thirst, let him come unto me and drink."* In John 4:14 Jesus accentuates the promise in the offer by using definite language of *"I shall give him"* and *"shall be in him a well of water springing up into everlasting life.*" This is clearly an offer to any and all of mankind to find salvation through Christ.

The necessity of acceptance to this offer is also unequivocally stated in scripture. Jesus, understanding that the strength of a covenant relationship would require a bilateral agreement, said in John 11:25, "*he that believeth in me though he were dead, yet shall he live.*" The acceptance to the offer is *believing.* If we do not believe, a covenant relationship cannot be developed. That is why believing on Christ is the foundation to a covenant relationship.

An acceptance to an offer also means a refusal to all other offers pertaining to the same agreement. If the subject matter is clearly defined, acceptance to an offer is exclusive to the terms of the accepted offer. Another example of this is the marriage covenant. When you say "I do" to your spouse you are saying "I don't" to all others.

Jesus Christ demands the same loyalty when you accept His offer of Salvation. In Matthew 10:37, Jesus says "*He that loveth father or mother more than me is not worthy of me: and he that loveth son or daughter more than me is not worthy of me.*" At first glance this may appear to be harsh, but upon further review we find that it is simply the formation of a legal covenant agreement.

Acceptance to the offer of Salvation from Christ requires exclusive acceptance and commitment.

Jesus elaborated on this principle in Mathew 6:24 when He stated that "*No man can serve two masters: for either he will hate the one, and love the other; or else he will hold to the one, and despise the other. Ye cannot serve God and mammon.*" Acceptance to the offer of Salvation from Christ requires exclusive acceptance and commitment. The legal nature of God requires it.

Offer and acceptance can become more intricate when trying to determine when an official offer or acceptance has taken place. Does it take place at the point of dispatch or at the point of receipt? Though modern email has changed the urgency of this clarity, an old common law came up with a rule called the mailbox rule. **The mailbox rule basically stated that the official offer or acceptance is when it has been dispatched rather than when it has been received.**

The Bible states in Romans 10:13, "*For whosoever shall call upon the name of the Lord shall be saved.*" Whenever you initiate the acceptance by calling on the Lord the offer of salvation is accepted. The excitement of this revelation places salvation in the grasp of every human being.

Romans chapter 10 goes on to say "*How then shall they call on him in whom they have not believed? And how shall they believe in him of whom they have not heard? And how shall they hear without a preacher? And how shall they preach, except they are sent?*" This process of being sent and being received clearly shows how God makes an offer through the declared Word of a messenger, and then humanity responds by declaring acceptance.

God in his infinite wisdom has established channels whereby man could enter a covenant agreement with deity. These channels are not just legal in nature, they are sure and established. They are tested by time and experience. The call goes out every day all over the world. The offer is dispatched. Man can immediately respond by calling on the Lord and accepting the offer to be a disciple of Christ.

CHAPTER FOURTEEN
Detrimental Reliance

❖

Contract law by its very nature looks for different ways to interpret the intent of the contracting parties. It seeks to make an injustice right by legal concepts and language that enforces that original intent. The different scenarios that contracts create are without number. Contract law seeks to use guidelines of principle and uniformity that will allow each of these different scenarios to be fairly judged and enforced if necessary.

One of the guidelines that evolved from the continual interpretation of contracts was a form of consideration called detrimental reliance. We know that every contract requires consideration, but we also know that consideration is not necessarily money. **The principle of detrimental reliance states that if one of the contracting parties relies on the promise of the other contracting party to his or her detriment, then adequate consideration has been given to make the contract enforceable.**

Detrimental reliance can occur in many forms, but it is most recognizable when one contracting party incurs debt in anticipation of the other party's performance. This debt has in effect bound the opposite party to fulfill their end of the agreement. If the agreement is breached then the party incurring the detrimental reliance has legal recourse.

The groundwork for understanding the detrimental reliance that our Savior incurred in anticipation of our performance is found in John 15:13 when Jesus is quoted as saying, *"Greater love hath no man than this, that a man lay down his life for his friends."*

The sacrifice is undisputed, but was the sacrifice a gift in anticipation of our performance? (In this case,

God gave us life, and when we breathe our first breath, we have entered into a covenant agreement with our Creator.

performance is our accepting the fact that Jesus' blood can wash away our sins and cleanse us if we ask for forgiveness and turn from our sinful ways.) The following verse, John 15:14, answers this question. *"Ye are my friends, if ye do whatsoever I command you."*

Jesus understood the price and the purpose of going to Calvary. He also fulfilled His end of the agreement in advance. He entered into covenant agreement with us before we were even born. This is why He has legal recourse to judge us if we reject Calvary and breach the agreement.

I am sure you have heard some question whether God will indeed judge humanity. This uncertainty also brings into question, what right does God have to judge me? God gave us life, and when we breathe our first breath, we have entered into a covenant agreement with our Creator. The right of God to judge us is brought into question by disputing the creation account of Genesis and the propagation of the theory of evolution.

Some may reason: If I don't believe that God created me, that gives me, in my humanity, an escape clause of accountability. This false sense of security will not save us from the legal right of God's judgment. When the Word, or essence of God, was made flesh according to John 1:2 and that flesh, Jesus, went willingly to Calvary, the new covenant brought into the agreement, a form of forbearance that we call detrimental reliance.

Calvary by its very nature was the detrimental reliance of a righteous God.

In Revelation 5, when we get a look into heaven and see the judgment seat where humanity is being tried, we find that the One that sits on the throne and has the authority to judge is described as *"a lamb that was slain, the Lion of the tribe of Judah and the root of David."* Revelation 5:9 goes further to confirm the identity of this judge by saying *"thou hast redeemed us to God by thy blood."* This is clearly the fleshly manifestation of the Son of God: Jesus.

No one among all of heaven and earth had the "legal right" to judge. The Bible describes it as *"no one was found worthy."* (Revelation 5:4) There is only one who has the authority to enforce the covenant agreement. Even if we don't believe that we were created by God, we will not have an excuse on judgment day. We will still be in breach of contract by rejecting Jesus. Calvary by its very nature was the detrimental reliance of a righteous God.

CHAPTER FIFTEEN
Promissory Estoppel

❖

Our nature may struggle with understanding and accepting that Jesus has the legal right to judge us through the legal right of Calvary when "we" did not enter into a traditional bargain for exchange. In other words, if we did not ask Jesus to go to Calvary, and we had nothing to do with the fact that Jesus went to Calvary, how does that action obligate us to contractual compliance?

In the 20th Century a legal doctrine was developed called promissory estoppel. It basically states that the traditional requirement of *bargained for consideration* is not necessary for a binding agreement if the promise would reasonably induce action or forbearance, and injustice could only be avoided by the enforcement of the promise.

This is often seen in pension cases when a pension is promised to an employee and at the time of fruition the promise is not honored. The law says that the nullification of that promise is "stopped." The promise must be honored even though traditional consideration is not a part of the agreement. Though this doctrine is still evolving in our courts, it serves to show a legal balancing act between the enforcement of a promise when the promisor and the promisee have not necessarily bargained for the desired result.

Consider the application of this doctrine to our covenant agreement with Jesus through Calvary. No doubt that a promise of salvation was included in the actions of Jesus at Calvary. The good news for us is that our enemy cannot nullify the effect of Calvary in our life. The blood of Jesus is more powerful than any unclean spirit or force of darkness. The enemy cannot "stop" the promises of God in your life without your consent.

The enemy cannot "stop" the promises of God in your life without your consent.

I quickly add that since promissory estoppel is an equitable remedy, and is used only as a last result, the plaintiff must have "clean hands" and must not have created the situation that he now complains of in his complaint. *Greiner v. Greiner, Kan. Sup. Ct.,* 131 Kan.

Unforgiven sin will compromise your case.

760, 293 (1930). If we are going to use the law to make our case in the court of spiritual powers, we better make sure we have the moral authority of a clean heart. Unforgiven sin will compromise your case.

This principle is clearly seen in Matthew 5:23-24 when Jesus instructed, *"Therefore if thou bring thy gift to the altar, and there rememberest that thy brother hath ought against thee; Leave there thy gift before the altar, and go thy way; first be reconciled to thy brother, and then come and offer thy gift."* The unclean hands of unforgiveness made the gift or petition of none effect.

It can also be said that such an action (Calvary) would reasonable induce action on our part. If a friend of yours gave his life for you, it seems reasonable that you would feel indebted and attempt to pay the debt through your kindness to his or her heirs. Even if the death was not the result of a promise, it is reasonable to assume some action on the part of the recipient.

The doctrine of promissory estoppel requires that you prove the injustice can only be avoided by the enforcement of the promise. The injustice of rejecting the one who gave His life for you is a part of the equation of Calvary. We are without excuse. We are bound by the dictates of our heart and the realm of legal precepts to give our life to God.

CHAPTER SIXTEEN
Statute of Frauds

❖

We often hear friends or parents say, "Always make sure you get it in writing." The idea that one can enforce an agreement easier if it is in writing comes from the statute of frauds.

The statute of frauds says that certain contracts must be in writing to be enforceable. Most statutes are patterned after the English statute enacted in 1677. The contracts that **must** be in writing are contracts that answer a creditor for the debt of another, marriage contracts, contracts for the sale of land or any interest in land, and contracts not to be performed within one year of the formation of the agreement.

The Uniform Commercial Code later added another category to the English statute that included a sale of goods where the contract price exceeded five hundred dollars. Rather than try to remember each type of contract that would be included in the statute, a rule of thumb was given for all agreements, "make sure you get it in writing."

Long before 1677, the Bible gives us some interesting examples of how the Lord dealt with the idea that things need to be in writing. One of the first examples we see of the legal nature of God as it pertains to writing down an agreement is when He wrote the ten commandments in stone (Exodus 34). God was not negotiating these laws; He was intending that they have the weight of a legal basis for enforcement capacity.

In Deuteronomy 6, God told Moses to have Israel write down these words *"that I command you"* on the posts of your house and on your gates. These words included such important truths like, *"Hear, O Israel: the LORD our God is one LORD."* Earlier, the Lord

The laws that govern our nation and our world are based on God's laws.

had mentioned that these truths shall be in their heart, but then an additional layer of importance was communicated when it was commanded that they be written down.

The Lord also commanded Moses in Exodus 17:14 to *"Write these words in a book for a memorial and rehearse it in the ears of Joshua."* It would seem that the writing down of these laws was for the purpose of remembrance and significance. **If the authors of the English common law saw the importance of putting the agreement in writing, then they were following a precedent that God had set in order years before.**

Isaiah 30:8 says: *"Now go, write it before them in a table, and note it in a book that it may be for the time to come for ever and ever."* The reason that writing it down is significant is because the Lord underscored its importance repeatedly in scripture. Our governmental laws followed suit with the Word of God. Yet many believe that the Bible is suspect and cannot be trusted. Meanwhile the laws that govern our nation and our world are based on God's laws.

It seems more than just coincidental that the specific areas of agreement that the common law put in the statute, that required the agreement to be written down, were also areas that the *God put flesh on the spoken Word.* Lord had already made provision for with instructions that the agreement or transaction be written down. The transfer of land or real property was spoken of in Jeremiah 32:10-11, the marriage agreement being dissolved by writing in Deuteronomy 24, and the settlement of a debt in Luke 16:5-7.

The importance of a covenant agreement between God and His people even fulfilled the statute of frauds in Jeremiah 31:33, *"but this shall be the covenant that I will make with the house of Israel; After those days, saith the LORD, I will put my law in their inward parts, and write it in their hearts; and will be their God, and they shall be my people."*

John tells us in the first chapter of the gospel that bears his name, *"In the beginning was the Word and the Word was with God and the Word was God. And the Word was made flesh and dwelt among us."* This Word refers to the creative spoken Word of God's nature. God put flesh on the spoken Word. This is the epitome of His nature; to take the power of an omniscience God and make it reachable and touchable.

God did not allow His Word to remain in spoken form alone. He has been writing it down for many years. God has encouraged others to "write it down." In Revelation 14 we read the testimony of John, *"and I heard a voice from heaven saying unto me, Write."* The Holy Spirit moved on men and they wrote. We have the Holy Bible that we hold in our hands as a constant reminder that God put the promises, the blessings, and the covenant in writing.

To make things more interesting, the Uniform Commercial Code has an exemption to the statute of frauds that applies to a sale of goods that would normally fall under the statute (price exceeds 500 dollars). Acceptance of part or all of the goods by the buyer, or payment of all or part of the purchase price by the buyer suffices as part performance to that portion of the contact; eliminating the need for formal statute of frauds adherence or does not have to be in writing to be enforced.

God has given us an earnest on our inheritance.

Humanity may feel they have an escape clause in the necessity for all of us to give our heart to God and follow the teaching of His Word. Some may say that because they did not put anything down in writing they are not required to give an account to God for their actions. **The problem with that reasoning is that we are already enjoying partial performance of the agreement.** He created the air that we breathe. He created the bodies that we are using to live life. We have accepted at least part of His goods to humanity.

For those that know the joy of living in His presence and being led by His Spirit, we are even further into the agreement. We have tasted of heavenly gifts. God has given us an earnest on our inheritance. Not only have we participated in the joy of this life, but also of the life to come. The written Word of God. The Spirit of God that is written on our hearts. The gifts of God as partial performance. All of these leave us without excuse and without escape.

CHAPTER SEVENTEEN
Statute of Limitations

❖

Virtually all actions at law whether civil or criminal have a statutory time beyond which the action may not be brought as a complaint in a court of law. If the statute runs and we do not bring our claim, then we are barred from being able to bring the claim at a later date. While there are exceptions to this law, like murder that generally has no statute of limitations, for the most part the law wants us to bring our claim or cause of action in a timely fashion.

One of the exciting aspects of God's promises is the seemingly lack of time limits. The promises that God made to Abraham or Moses thousands of years ago are still applicable today. The promise of the Holy Ghost to humanity in Acts 2:39 included language that would remove any limitation with the words, *"For this promise is to you and your children and to them that are afar off, even as many as the Lord our God shall call."*

Once the law had been signed and the purpose of that law had run, it could not be reversed or revisited. This in effect created a statute of limitations.

Other scriptures indicate that there may be certain time frames that are critical for the fulfillment of God's promises. In speaking of Esau in Hebrews 12:17 the scripture says *"For ye know how that afterward, when he would have inherited the blessing, he was rejected: for he found no place of repentance, though he sought it carefully with tears."* Apparently after Esau rejected the birthright and his brother Jacob took it, there was no revocation of that blessing.

The scripture also refers to an irrevocable law that Daniel faced in the book of Daniel, chapter six. King Darius was forced to throw Daniel in a den of lions that he did not favor doing, but nonetheless was bound by his own law. Certain laws of God and of man, especially from the Old Testament, will not accommodate a future claim to be filed or granted. Once the law had been signed and the purpose of that law had run, it could not be reversed or revisited. This in effect created a statute of limitations.

The scripture goes on to mention a *"time of trouble,"* a *"time of harvest,"* a *"time of healing,"* a *"time of need,"* and a *"time of love."* The book of Acts then mentions a *"time of promise"* in Acts 7:17. If God does not have a need of time and is not bound by time, then how does time figure into the framework of God's promises in our life? The answer is once again found in the legal nature of God.

God created time for the purpose of governing His creation. The seasons are simply blocks of time. The solar day and even the lunar night while serving the purpose of light are specific measurements of time. In a natural world with natural laws, time is of the essence. **Man became more subject to time when sin entered the human race.** While God is not bound by time, He uses time to corral us and to coax us. Just as God follows His own laws, he also uses the laws of time for our benefit.

While God is not bound by time, He uses time to corral us and to coax us.

We are famous for procrastinating. We have to discipline ourselves to not put off for tomorrow what we can do today. Can you imagine what we would be like with no laws of time? The boundaries of time removed. We may get a glimpse of this when we vacation and can't seem to remember what day of the week it is. This seems great for a while, but then it can become a little disorienting.

We start to feel like we are not in control of our world. We start to feel like we are adrift with no distinct markers. In reality, we are not ultimately in control of our world, but God gives us time to measure and to mark. He does not need time, but He gives us time so that we can function more effectively with this limited nature that we are carrying around. For God, time is a tool.

Consider what Barron's Law Dictionary, Third Edition, says about the statute of limitations: "The policy underlying the enactment of such laws concerns the belief that there is a point beyond which a prospective defendant should no longer need to worry about the possible commencement in the future of an action against him or her, that the law disfavors stale evidence and that no one should be able to sit on his rights for an unreasonable amount of time without forfeiting his or her claims."

The laws of man through the stature of limitations believes that time should be used as a relief. Even if we do something wrong, there should be a point at which we no longer have to live under the curse or the fear of the wrong. If man offers this relief through a law, don't you think that God, the inventor of time, has an even better system in place?

God puts his promises within the context of time when man is required to act on the promises. "*A place of repentance*" requires us to act upon the requirement of asking and then turning. The forgiving power of God is without limitation and without time constraints because the blood of Calvary is a supernatural act. Esau sought repentance carefully with tears, but before the cleansing blood of Calvary, the law did not allow turning to God in our own time frame.

Our burdens are limited by time, but our blessings from God are without limitation.

The legal nature of God gave us time to mark our sorrows, our hurts, our fears and our tears. He used time to remind us that our troubles are only temporary. Psalms 30:5 says "*Weeping may endure for a night but joy cometh in the morning.*" Our burdens are limited by time, but our blessings from God are without limitation.

The Holy Ghost is a supernatural gift from God that is without limitation, yet the Bible states in John 7:39 that the infilling of the Holy Ghost could not begin until Jesus was glorified or ascended into heaven. The outpouring of the Holy Ghost was dependent on the resurrection and ascension of Jesus and the resurrection of Christ were dependent on the crucifixion. **Thus, the initial outpouring of God's Spirit was governed by time, but once it was given, then the unlimited nature of God made the promise without limits.**

If the people in Noah's generation had a limited time to get on the ark, and if we have a limited time to prepare for the second coming of the Lord, then perhaps there is a clue given in the law that "no one should be able to sit on his rights for an unreasonable amount of time without forfeiting his or her claims." The tension between our limited time and God's unlimited love should provide encouragement and prompt us with a sense of urgency.

THE TRIAL

We have an Advocate...and
He is also the Judge

❖

In the summer of 1997, I accepted an offer to study at Oxford University; just a short drive from London, England. The program I studied in was a comparative law program that compared the laws of England to the laws of the United States; particularly in the area of criminal procedures. I arrived at the campus of Magdalen College in Oxford, England on a crisp day in early June. The Oxford University is made up of 38 independent college campuses in the city of Oxford. I was fortunate to be at one of the more beautiful campuses on the Cherwell River.

One of my professors at Oxford was the Honorable Stephen Thayer III, who at the time was a State Supreme Court justice from the state of New Hampshire. Judge Thayer had been a federal prosecutor prior to his appointment to the bench. He was very well-versed in trial law and had never lost a case. We knew he would be a wealth of information. Judge Thayer explained to us early on that when a lawyer says he has never lost a case it is because he only took the cases that he knew he could win.

I thought about how that Jesus has never lost one battle. Not one contest. Not one conflict. He is undefeated in every trial. And He doesn't just take the easy ones; He took on the most difficult of all trials. The trial of sin. The trial of death. The trial of hell. His ways really are above our ways and His thoughts really are above our thoughts (Isaiah 55:9).

Judge Thayer shared with us some of the gamesmanship and strategy of trial law. Trial law is like a big chess game where the components have to move into the right places at the right time to ensure victory. There are many moving pieces during a trial and the attorneys are like generals moving their little army into strategic locations. The idea of putting your case before the jury, a judge, and cross examination is that the fire of scrutiny will cause the truth to rise to the surface. Whatever is not accurate or logical will evaporate under the hot glare of questioning. This may or may not happen in modern jurisprudence, but that is the philosophy behind the oral arguments of trial law.

This philosophy of trial by fire resonated in my mind as I thought about the trials of faith that many of the early Christians endured. If anything has been tested over the years by persecution, it is the faith of God's people. I once heard Larry King, the famous television and radio personality, interviewing Charles Colson. Charles Colson was in President Richard Nixon's White House as a member of his legal team and got caught up in Watergate, the break in and cover-up scandal that forced President Nixon to resign. In 1973, Mr. Colson converted to Christianity and voluntarily pled guilty to an obstruction of justice charge in 1974. After serving seven months in prison, Mr. Colson started Prison Fellowship in 1976. The ministry has grown to the world's largest outreach to prisoners, ex-prisoners, crime victims and their families with 40,000 volunteers in 113 countries.

Larry King asked Mr. Colson, "How do you know that Jesus is really the Son of God?" Mr. Colson said. "Because of the faith of His disciples, the post Apostolic fathers and the early Christians. Many of these gave their life for the gospel. If Jesus was not the Son of God, why would they lay down their life for such a man?" Mr. Colson went on to explain, "I saw firsthand how men abandoned the President when it was clear that the Nixon administration was going down. They were like rats running off a sinking ship." Mr. Colson said. "If men would abandon a President, don't you think the disciples would have saved their own necks if they knew that Jesus was a phony?" It was an irrefutable point.

Christianity is not unaware of the trial of fire. It is something that has been a part of molding the faith of believers for centuries and yet the truth continues to rise to the top. At the time, I did not know that John Foxe who wrote *Foxe's Book of Martyrs*, a famous book about the early Christians that gave their life for the gospel, wrote his manuscripts while sitting in the old library of Magdalen College in Oxford.

CHAPTER EIGHTEEN
Preserving the Issue of Salvation

❖

Judge Thayer taught us that it was important to raise the issue at the trial level so that the issue is preserved in case you decide to appeal. There is a trial procedure rule that says, one cannot appeal an issue that was not raised at the trial level. It is not enough to raise the issue in a pre-trial motion like a motion to suppress evidence; it must also be raised at the trial level for the issue to be preserved. If one does not preserve the issue, the Appellant judges cannot hear the appeal on the issue even though they may agree with the protest. **"It is the single biggest mistake that lawyers make in trial," Judge Thayer informed us.**

On a rainy July afternoon, the president of Magdalen College, Anthony Smith, gave several of us law students a private tour of some fascinating works of art. We went into a sealed library where the public is not allowed. This library was constructed when the college was founded in 1458.

As we strolled through the old library, Mr. Smith showed us where John Foxe wrote his famous Foxe's Book of Martyrs. With millions of copies in print, this exceptional historical record traces the roots of religious persecution through the sixteenth century. It examines the heroic lives of great men and women such as John Hus, John Wycliffe, William Tyndale, Anne Askew, Lady Jane Grey, and Martin Luther.

John Foxe also knew persecution. Forced to flee from his native England during Queen Mary's severe persecution of those holding reformed views, he carefully compiled records of martyred Christians. His writings possess a sense of immediacy and insight into suffering that few "objective" church historians can match. It seemed strange that he sat right where we were standing and compiled these accounts even while his life was being threatened.

I saw pieces of the original work of St. John written in 60 A.D. The pieces contain 14 words describing the anointment of Jesus' feet by Mary Magdalene. Apparently, the work had been given to Magdalen College in Oxford since the school was named after Mary Magdalene in the Bible.

The president asked me to accompany him into a small air conditioned chamber with low lights. I helped him carry some carefully wrapped boxes. Only later when we opened them for the others to see, did I realize I was carrying the original work of Sir Lawrence of Arabia. Sir Lawrence toured the Middle East region and drew large maps of the area. I carried another book that had been written only 60 years after the invention of the printing press in the 10th century.

The greatest treasure and the most prized possession of Oxford University is what we saw next. A slab of stone with the carved image of King Ahaserarus of Media Persia from the Biblical book of Esther was standing before us. It contained an inscription that read, "I am the King of Kings." This was carved at the instruction of the king and is 2600 years old. It is the oldest original inscription that we have and it was written in Arabic.

In the chapel we saw a copy of Leonardo Da Vinci's, *The Last Supper*, drawn by one of his students. Located only 10 years prior, this master-piece had been rolled up in a storage area at the Royal Academy of Art. I walked away thinking about how our greatest works of art can be lost if not properly preserved. **Not only is this preservation necessary in a physical sense, it is critical that the spiritual issues be preserved for generations to come.** The only way that these issues will be preserved is if we raise them now. We must raise them early on and often. We have Biblical precedent for such a practice.

God wanted to make sure that the issue or benefit of the Law was preserved.

1. The Word of God

In the book of Joshua, we find three different issues that the Lord instructed Joshua to preserve. The first is the issue of the book of the Law. It was important to God that the Old Testament Law would not depart or be lost on the sea of time. God instructed Joshua to *"not let the Law depart out of your mouth"* (Joshua 1:8). In other words, keep talking about it. Keep raising the issue. He also instructed Joshua in the same verse to "*meditate*" on it. Keep it in your mind. Talk about it and think about it. God then told Joshua to "*observe*" it. That means do it. Live it! God told Joshua to observe *all* of the written book.

If God is concerned about preserving the issue in terms of His Word, then this period of time that Joshua lived was crucial for the record to be preserved. The Pentateuch is the period of time when the Law was given to Moses. The post Pentateuch period is when the Children of Israel were moving to a new land and making a new start. **God wanted to make sure that the issue or benefit of the Law was preserved because he was planning on it being a part of their future and not just their past.**

This same principle was observed in the New Testament as well. Paul said in I Corinthians 14:37, "*If any man think himself to be a prophet, or spiritual, let him acknowledge that the things that I write unto you are the commandments of the Lord.*" Peter said in II Peter 1:20-21, "*Knowing this first, that no prophecy of the scripture is of any private interpretation. For the prophecy came not in old time by the will of man: but holy men of God spoke as they were moved by the Holy Ghost.*"

There is a thread of consistency from the Old Testament to the New Testament to modern times that the Word of God must be preserved. This Word must be preserved because it will be the standard that God uses when he judges all of humanity in that final day. The Supreme Court of all Supreme Courts. Revelation 20 describes this as the judgment at the great white throne.

This Word must be preserved because it will be the standard that God uses when he judges all of humanity in that final day.

The Book of Kells at Trinity College in Dublin, Ireland is nearly 900 years old and well preserved. The Book of Kells contains the complete writings of the four gospels. They were handwritten by monks in the city of Kell and preserved through fire, water, and captivity. They were rolled up in someone's house and in the basement of an old cathedral, but well preserved after all of these years. More amazing is the fact that the Book of Kells is a perfect and complete translation in accordance with our King James Version of the four gospels of the New Testament.

The written record of His Word has been preserved all of these years, so we can read a promise from the Bible and it is applicable to our lives. It is valid. The Word of God can not only be raised in reference to the modern issues that you face, but it has the legal authority to be a prevailing authority in your life. All other authority has to bow to the Book.

2.   The Power of God

The second issue that Joshua was instructed to preserve was the power of God. God could preserve His power without Joshua, but God wanted Joshua to keep the power of God present before the people. The Lord parts the Jordan River just as he did the Red Sea (Joshua 4:23). Why did He do that? Is this the only miracle that God knows how to do? No, God desired to remind the next generation that his power had not changed. God wanted them to see that the power was preserved. The trials of the desert had not diminished God's power.

The power of God is not in anything or anyone independent of God. It is the same power through the whole Bible. Jesus preserved the issue in Matthew 28:18 when He said, "*all power is given unto me in heaven and earth.*" The same power that was on display at the time of Moses and Joshua was preserved at the trial level of Jesus' ministry. This power was preserved so that in Romans 1:8 the same power would still be present when Jesus said, "*Ye shall receive power after that the Holy Ghost is come upon you.*"

The power of God has been preserved all of these years so the church would have the authority to raise the issue to a generation of people that need to know that God's power can make a difference in their life. This world is not interested in some powerless religion. Just going through the motions leaves people empty and void, but the issue of supernatural power has been preserved so that God can change our life and make the impossible, possible.

3.   The Person of God

The third issue that was preserved with Joshua was that of a supernatural leader. In Joshua 5:14, God appeared unto Joshua saying "*as the Captain of the Host of the Lord and I now come.*" God said to Moses in Exodus 3:5 that He was "*I AM*". In Exodus 3:6 God said "*I am the God of Abraham, Issac, and Jacob.*" In I Corinthians 10:4, Paul said in reference to the children of Israel in the wilderness, "*...and drank the* *same spiritual drink; for they drank from the spiritual rock that accompanied them, and that rock was Christ."*

The one who was in the wilderness as I AM and the one who stood before Joshua as CAPTAIN OF THE HOST, is the one who came in the incarnation of JESUS CHRIST. **God has preserved the issue that His people would have a leader that was a supernatural demonstration of God.** The issue of manifestation in the form of a supernatural leader was brought to fruition in the life of Jesus Christ. That is why Jesus said, *"If you have seen me, you have seen the father."* (John 14:9).

Then came Calvary, and it appeared that the issue had not been preserved. The forces that opposed God did not understand that there was a principle at work. A stone was not going to stifle the plan of God. A cave could not contain this Savior. A tomb could not terminate God's purpose. The issue of Calvary could not be contained on a hill. The issue had been

A tomb could not terminate God's purpose.

preserved. The issue was raised in the royal court of God's providence and when it was, the objection was noted and a resurrection resulted.

CHAPTER NINETEEN
The Court of Last Resort

❖

A Writ of Habeas Corpus is often used in criminal court to determine the legality of someone's custody. Habeas Corpus is Latin for "We have the body." It can only be filed when the accused is in custody. **When a Writ of Habeas Corpus is filed, the court is asked to determine the legality of the confinement.** It is often the very first filing that an attorney does for a client that has been taken into custody. These types of writs are nicknamed Habs by the attorneys and while it may be perfunctory in nature, they are rooted in the Constitution and take precedence over local statutes and laws. In other words, a lesser power cannot usurp a greater power.

An interesting story is given to us in I Samuel 5. The Philistines were the chief nemesis for the Children of Israel. These countries were always fighting. When the Children of Israel were obeying God, they would win the skirmishes with the Philistines. When the Children of Israel were not obeying God, they were losing the battles to the Philistines. At the beginning of I Samuel, we see that the Children of Israel are in a backslidden state, and the Philistines are routing them in every battle. In one battle, someone in the Israel camp got the absurd idea to bring the Ark of the Covenant into the battlefield and force God to give them the victory. This did not work because man cannot force the hand of God. The Ark of the Covenant was taken captive by the Philistines.

A lesser power cannot hold a greater power in confinement.

The Philistines worshipped a god they called Dagon. Dagon was an idol that was supposedly half god and half fish. A temple to Dagon was built by the Philistines in the city of Ashdod. The Ark of the Covenant was brought by the Philistines to Ashdod and set before the statute of Dagon as if to say, "Our god is bigger than your God." However, the problem is God considers this an illegal confinement. A lesser power cannot hold a greater power in confinement.

The Ark of the Covenant was a representation of God's power and when it was put into Dagon's jail, natural law immediately determined that there was a problem. The custody violated the laws of nature. The creator was being held captive by the creation. When the priests of Dagon came into the temple, they noticed that the Dagon idol had fallen down with its face on the ground in front of the Ark. (I Samuel 5:3). The priests of Dagon set the idol back up, but when they came in the next day, they found the idol was toppled over again and the hands, feet, and even the head of the idol were cut off so that only a stump remained. (I Samuel 5:4).

God did not even need man to help Him. In God's court of justice, this illegal captivity cannot stand. There is no higher law than God's law, so God just turned the courtroom upside down. His Habeas Corpus was filed, granted, and enacted all in the same moment. This is the result of a lesser power illegally attempting to hold a greater power in confinement.

The body of Jesus was taken and placed in a tomb. The forces of evil said, *"We have the body."* The earth is now suppose to hold captive the fleshly manifestation of All Mighty God; the Son of God. This is an illegal confinement. The greater power is now being held by a lesser power. On the third day, the Habeus Corpus is granted and the body is released.

Sin will try to hold a child of God captive, but this is an illegal confinement. Sin says, *"I have the body,"* but a higher law says, *"You have the body illegally, turn loose."* If we are filled with the Spirit of God and sin tries to get a grip on us, we can file a spiritual Habeus Corpus and the lesser power of sin has to release the greater power of God's Spirit. That is why the Bible says, *"Greater is he that is in you, than he that is in the world."* (1 John 4:4).

There comes a time when the power from within demands a hearing.

Different things can hold our bodies captive. Some vice of the flesh that controls every waking moment. Some habit that we can't break. Some thought that keeps reoccurring in the night. It has a grip on us. Years ago, we became its captive. Perhaps we thought we would always be its slave, so we struggled silently, learning to live in an illegal captivity. However, there comes a time when the power from within demands a hearing. A protest is formulated. An Habeus Corpus is filed. The soul dares to believe its release is imminent. The appeal goes to the court of last resort, and the message comes booming back out of the clouds and into the crevices of the heart…"Let My People Go!"

The Children of Israel marched out of Egypt. Peter marched out of a darkened dungeon with chains dangling loose around his arms. The soul of a man or woman who feels the weight of sin removed starts to sing and rejoice. We sang a song in church when I was a kid that said, *"Once like a bird in prison I dwelt, no freedom from my sorrow I felt. But, Jesus came and listened to me and Glory to God, He set me free."*

The Psalmist David cried, *"Our soul is escaped as a bird out of the snare of the fowlers; the snare is broken and we are escaped."* (Psalms 124:7) Sometimes when you have battled long and hard and prayerfully with an evil thing, there comes a time when you suddenly realize that the pull of it, the lure and magnetism and fascination of it, are not there any longer. The snare is broken. The "bird" has escaped, your soul flies free.

The court of last resort is the highest court in the land. It is the court with the most authority in your particular case. In a state action, the court of last resort would be the State Supreme Court where the action was filed. In a federal court, the court of last resort would be the U.S. Supreme Court. In a spiritual protest, the court of last resort is God's court of justice. It is the court that hears all matters relating to the soul. It is the court that oversees every other court.

Regardless of what the final outcome is in man's reasoning, you still have an appeal to a higher court.

If your boss is not treating you fairly, appeal to God's court of last resort. If your spouse is not faithful, appeal to the court of last resort. If you have a battle that you are facing that is bigger than you are, appeal to the court of last resort. If your body is broken and the doctors say they can't help you, appeal to the court of last resort. Regardless of what the final outcome is in man's reasoning, you still have an appeal to a higher court.

The Dagon statute was not able to keep his head, his hands, or his feet. He fell on his face before the Ark of the Covenant. He could not keep his head on straight. He lost his mind. Dagon's missing hands and feet were symbolic of his lack of power to work in lives. He did not have any mobility. I have been to museums in Europe where all of the statutes had their heads and hands removed. This was performed by conquering nations to remove the faith that the people had in their gods.

God is clear in His message to His people that there is *"no weapon formed against you that will prosper."* (Isaiah 54:17). The head is the control center, so when you consider that the head of your enemy is no match for the will of God, you can also recognize that your own control center must be in God's will and not your will alone. **You can take off your hat when you come into God's presence as a sign of reverence, but if you linger in His presence your bowing turns to breaking.**

A Federal Habeas Corpus cannot be filed until all the remedies under state law have been exhausted. This is called a Writ of Last Resort. Sometimes we must exhaust all of our options before we can recognize our need of release from the prison called sin. The good news is that the court of last resort has all of the authority. Regardless of how many times we have lost at lower trials, the court of last resort can overturn them all.

CHAPTER TWENTY
Beyond a Reasonable Doubt

❖

While attending Oxford University, I was asked to pray before a formal meal at one of the Inns of Court in London. The meal was quite formal with each of us wearing robes. Several judges from the Queen's Bench were expected, and I was excited about the opportunity to say grace prior to the meal. I was instructed before the meal that it would be best for me not to pray in Jesus name because it might be offensive to some, and then I was told that even praying to the Father might be offensive. I suggested (tongue in cheek) that maybe I should address my prayer "To whom it may concern." The instructors thought I was serious and were just delighted with this suggestion.

We gathered in this great hall. A hall with a history of several hundred years. We all had our robes on as the custom is in England. The formality and pageantry of the English legal society is quite enjoyable. I was seated at the main table and when the appropriate time came, I was introduced with great English flair that makes one believe someone important is about to speak. Attempting to continue with this formality, I rose slowly and then in my best English accent I drawled out, "Let us please bow our heads." After giving the audience a considerable pause so the weight of the moment could be measured, I lifted my hands up toward heaven and announced with a loud booming American voice, "Dear Jesus, our Heavenly Father, we are thankful for this gathering...."

I could feel some of the eyes looking around and maybe even some wary glances of concern, but I did not want to be derelict in my duties of being a witness. If the name of Jesus was not allowed to be uttered in that hall, I would not be a co-cospirator of silence. I did not want there to be any doubt that I was addressing my prayer to Jesus and besides, it was kind of fun to throw a little American independence into the

English formalism. Sometimes we are forced into being camouflage Christians, but I believe that we should let our faith resonate to the point that we are clearly, beyond a reasonable doubt, proclaiming the gospel.

Beyond a reasonable doubt is a standard of proof that is necessary to achieve when convicting a defendant in a criminal trial. No one has put a percentage on it, but it is considered to be close to overwhelming evidence. The proof is so conclusive and complete that all reasonable doubts of the fact are removed from the mind of the ordinary person.

A civil trial is much different; the weight of evidence only has to be the preponderance of guilt for a defendant to be convicted. Preponderance of evidence is 51% or more evidence against a defendant than for a defendant in order for a conviction to be valid. A higher standard is used in criminal law because the punishment is greater.

In Acts 26, we read a compelling story about the Apostle Paul witnessing to the Roman governor, Festus, and the Jewish king under the Roman Empire, Agrippa. Apparently, Paul was quite anointed in his testifying because at one point the Roman governor spoke to Paul and told him, *"much learning hath made thee mad."* (Acts 26:24). Towards the conclusion of the testimony, King Agrippa said to Paul, *"Almost thou persuadest me to be a Christian."* (Acts 26:28). King Agrippa knew what Paul was saying was truth, but perhaps he did not want to convert because of the lifestyle change that would be required or the peer pressure with the Roman governor present. Whatever the excuse, it was not enough courage or conviction to overcome the reasonable doubt mark.

Proof is illusive when it is examined under the microscope of reason and logic. Books confer and contradict. Scholars theorize and hypothesize through the paradigm of personal interpretation. But when you cut through all the opinions and all the ideas, there is one thing that tips the scales, so that the proof slides beyond a reasonable doubt. The answer is found in the following verse when Paul answered King Agrippa. Paul said, *"I would to God, that not only thou, but also all that hear me this day, were both almost and altogether such as I am, except these bonds."* (Acts 28:29).

Proof is illusive when it is examined under the microscope of reason and logic.

Paul was saying that *almost* is good, but must be combined with *altogether* to move us from complacency to commitment. *Almost* may get our attention, but God wants our heart. God wants to know that our faith is beyond a reasonable doubt. *Almost* may get us to preponderance under a civil trial standard, but *beyond a reasonable doubt* will get us to an altar of repentance. Paul made it clear that it comes down to a personal experience: Do you know him for yourself? Paul had a personal experience with Christ, and he wished that for everyone. **Once we have a personal experience with Christ, we believe in him beyond a reasonable doubt**.

I repeatedly heard that it was an incredible experience to parachute out of a plane. I enjoyed the stories, but felt that there was no reason to jump out of a perfectly safe airplane. I was doubtful that anything was worth the risk of trusting your life to a big kite and some ropes. So, I listened to the tales and only smiled. However, I wondered what it would be like to freefall for a mile in the air. One day, I decided I was going to experience it for myself. With an instructor strapped to me, I jumped out of a plane two miles over the desert. Now, I can say beyond a reasonable doubt, it is quite an experience. What I can't say beyond a reasonable doubt is that I would ever do it again.

After praying at the Inns of the Court in London in Jesus' name, one of the instructors came back to the rear of the bus that many of us students were on as we rode back to Oxford. We laughed about me taking my liberty of praying and the reaction of the judges. Then the instructor asked me, "Are you filled with the Holy Spirit?" I confirmed that I was and he said, "How do you know that your experience is real and not fake?"

"Because I have experienced it," I explained.

When you have experienced something you are in a better position than anyone else to determine the validity or truthfulness of that experience.

In Acts 4, the religious leaders questioned Peter and John because of their boldness to proclaim Christ. They realized that this boldness did not come from higher education or from a position of prestige, but rather from the fact that they had been with Jesus. (Acts 4:13). Even people that were opposed to the gospel being preached recognized that a personable experience gives you boldness beyond a reasonable doubt.

Jesus offers an undeniable experience that is beyond a reasonable doubt.

As the council tried to decide what to do with Peter and John, they reached a conclusion that is rooted in logic. A man who had been lame and sat at

82

the gate of the temple all of his life was now healed and was jumping and dancing around in the temple. The council came to the right conclusion that this miracle was not anything they could deny. (Acts 4:16). They were right because there were eyewitnesses at the temple. Many people were part of this miraculous experience. It matters not what punishment or law you want to put on it to try and limit the impact, the bottom line is that Jesus offers an undeniable experience that is beyond a reasonable doubt.

You have probably heard the question, "If you were on trial for being a Christian would there be enough evidence to convict you?" You now know after reading this book that you can respond by asking, "Civil or criminal court?" No really, we should always have our faith so firmly planted in our hearts, that there is no doubt of where we stand. Maybe a better question would be, **"Is there enough evidence in the life, trial, death and resurrection of Jesus Christ to overcome any reasonable doubt as to who Christ is?"** If there isn't, then only a personal experience with Christ will override any lingering doubt.

The Bible says it this way, *"A fool hath said in his heart, there is no God."* (Psalms 14:1) In other words, there is enough evidence in just the natural world, to convince any human beyond a reasonable doubt that there is a God. Doubt diminishes in the experience. Reasonable doubt is lost in the ocean of humanity shouting: *"Holy is the Lamb slain from the foundation of the world."* A personal experience trumps the theories of a thousand men.

A personal experience trumps the theories of a thousand men.

CHAPTER TWENTY-ONE
The Right of Counsel

❖

It's reported that in Charlotte, North Carolina, a secular lawyer purchased a box of very rare and expensive cigars, then insured them against, among other things, fire. Within a month, having smoked his entire stockpile of these cigars, the lawyer filed a claim against the insurance company. In his claim, the lawyer stated the cigars were lost "in a series of small fires." The insurance company refused to pay, citing the obvious reason, that the man had consumed the cigars in the normal fashion. The lawyer sued and won!

Delivering the ruling, the judge agreed with the insurance company that the claim was frivolous. The judge stated, nevertheless, that the lawyer held a policy from the company, in which it had warranted that the cigars were insurable and also guaranteed that it would insure them against fire, without defining what is considered to be unacceptable "fire." Consequently, the insurance company was obligated to pay the claim.

Rather than endure a lengthy and costly appeal process, the insurance company accepted the ruling and paid $15,000 to the lawyer for his loss of the cigars that perished in the "fires." After the lawyer cashed the check, the insurance company had him arrested on 24 counts of arson! With his insurance claim and testimony from the previous case being used against him, the lawyer was convicted of intentionally burning his insured property and was sentenced to 24 months in jail and a $24,000 fine.

The law guarantees you a right to counsel, but it does not guarantee you a right to good counsel. According to the 6th amendment of the United States Constitution, in all criminal prosecutions, you shall enjoy the right of assistance of counsel for your defense. This law has evolved over the years. For many years testimony given without counsel was admitted into evidence so long as the testimony was voluntary and not the result of coercion.

In 1944, *Ashcraft v. Tennessee*, 322 U.S.143 (1944) provided testimony where a man was questioned for 36 hours without a break. The court held that this type of questioning without counsel was inherently coercive. From this case the U.S. Supreme Court developed the "inherent coerciveness rule." In 1963, the case *Gideon v. Wainwright*, 372 U.S. 335 (1963) stood for making the right of counsel obligatory on the states. The U.S. Supreme Court declared that it was impossible to have a fair trial without counsel.

In 1963, the case *Douglas v. California*, 372 U.S. 353 (1963) became the benchmark decision for determining that it was unconstitutional for the court to review the record and determine whether or not the defendant was in need of a court appointed attorney for the appeal process. Then came *Messiah v. United States*, 377 U.S. 201 (1964) where the court held that a defendant has a right to counsel from the point of formal indictment. This was followed by *Escobedo v. Illinois*, 378 U.S. 478 (1964) where it was determined that counsel was needed even before indictment.

The famous case of *Miranda v. Arizona*, 384 U.S. 436 (1966) stated that police must give a warning upon arrest by saying, "You have a right to remain silent, any statement you make can and will be used against you. You have a right to an attorney. If you cannot afford an attorney, one will be appointed for you." **In 1984, the case *Berkemer v. McCarty*, 468 U.S. 420 (1984) attempted to clarify when a custody arrest begins. It was determined that it begins when one's "freedom is curtailed."**

It makes one wonder if court appointed counsel would be necessary if people followed Biblical counsel, but it seems to be that the courts may have backed into something when they declared that counsel is required when "one's freedom is curtailed." There is no doubt that sin restricts a person's freedom. The Bible declares, "*If any man sin, we have an advocate.*" (I John 2:1) God gives us an advocate when our freedom is curtailed and possibly even before.

According to Webster's Dictionary, an advocate is one that "pleads the cause of another." In ancient Greece, an advocate was one who counseled, coached, and championed the cause of another in court. The New Testament Greek word for advocate is made up of two terms, "Para" meaning alongside and "Kaleo" meaning to call. Together, "Parakletos"

In ancient Greece, an advocate was one who counseled, coached, and championed the cause of another in court.

conveys the idea that one is called alongside to assist, defend, or intercede on behalf of another.

The only writer in all of scripture to use the term "Parakletos" is John. The Apostle uses the term repeatedly in chapters 13-17, in the Gospel that bears his name. In each case it refers to the Holy Spirit or the Holy Ghost, both terms meaning the same. This term is also used by John in the upper room discourse. When the disciples and Jesus were celebrating the Passover, the Lord knew that little time was left and when He was arrested, tried, and crucified, the disciples would be left alone. He knew they would be afraid. Jesus offered them assurance of the coming comforter.

In John 14:16 we read, *"And I will pray the father, and he shall give you another comforter, that he may abide with you forever."* In the King James Version, it says *"Comforter."* In the New International Version it says, *"Counselor."* All of the translations give perfect symmetry to the fact that the Holy Spirit is sent to help, comfort, and to counsel. Later in the Gospel, John expounds upon the role of this helper, *"But the Comforter, which is the Holy Ghost, whom the father will send in my name, he shall teach you all things, and bring all things to your remembrance, whatsoever I have said unto you."* (John 14:26).

The counsel that we receive is the Holy Ghost and this counsel is available when our freedom is curtailed. The Bible says that we are born in sin, (Romans 3:23), so we need this assistance from day one. We need an advocate from the very beginning of our life. Sometimes in our humanity we like to think that we do not need the Spirit of God in our life, but that would be similar to trying to defend our self in a criminal trial. I never have seen one of those situations come out well.

If you are going to have an advocate, you need a good one. A good attorney will keep you informed. He or she will tell you what is happening and what it means. You do not want an attorney that keeps you in the dark. John said, *"the Holy Ghost will teach you all things, and bring all things to your remembrance."* (John 14:26). That is a good advocate. One that will teach us and remind us. We need that every day of our life. We need a counselor that will make us aware of what opposing counsel is doing. The Holy Spirit reveals what the enemy is trying to do in our life.

The right to counsel is voluntary. It will not be forced on us. We are required by the laws of the land to inform of the availability of an advocate, but one can waive the right. The same is true of God in our lives. He does not force Himself or His Spirit onto humanity. He does not sneak up on an individual when he is not looking and jump in his heart. God has to be invited. He has to know that one desires His assistance. If a person doesn't want God, they can wave Him away. That is what having a free will is all about, but be aware of the consequences.

In my second year of law school, I joined the Moot Court team and soon learned that I loved presenting my case to a panel of judges. I would write a brief for and also against a pre-determined issue. Then I would argue for the issue and afterward against the issue. While making my case, the panel of judges would fire questions at me. The skill of oral arguments is to start out making your case, answer the judges' questions immediately as they ask them, then be able to seamlessly weave the questions back into your prepared statements without losing the thread of consistency. All of this happens very rapidly as you compete against other Moot Court teams from different law schools around the country.

The panel of judges graded me on my presentation and it is impossible to go into this arena without your adrenaline pumping and your heart racing with excitement. After one competition in which I felt like I had nailed the issues with passion and precision, I exited the courtroom and went around to the side of the building where no one was in ear shot and shouted to myself while pumping my fist in the air, "I was made for this." Immediately the Lord smote my heart and said, "No you were not. I created you to preach my gospel." I found myself calming down very quickly and asking God to forgive me. It is our nature to try and be our own advocate, but woe to the man that rejects the counsel of God.

CHAPTER TWENTY-TWO
The Public Defender

❖

Our Moot Court teams in law school competed effectively. Eventually, one competition pitted my partner and I against the National Champion Moot Court team of Stetson University Law School. We were competing in Orlando with the opportunity to have our final arguments debated before the Florida State Supreme Court. I was directly competing against a female debater that was well known in the Moot Court circles for her debating skills. She was well trained and very poised. I knew it was going to be a tough challenge. Our team presented and the opposing team rebutted. We then switched sides and argued the opposite positions.

The female presenter on the Stetson team skillfully directed her arguments and wove the judges' questions into her main position with no apparent gaps. The Stetson team in their matching navy blazers felt confident that they had the better argument, and their confidence bolstered their performance. I felt sure that we had also prepared well and were holding our own. We were defeated by the more experienced team from Stetson and after the decision was announced, the female debater from Stetson shook my hand and offered this backhanded compliment: "You were a worthy opponent."

I knew immediately that being a worthy opponent is not what anyone should aspire to. It rings of a consolation prize perhaps similar to: *"Thanks for playing, now Johnny has some nice departing gifts for you."* No one wants to hear those words. Especially if you are accused of a crime and your life is on the line. If the judge says you had adequate representation, but you are pronounced guilty, the adequate representation means little to nothing other than the fact that you will have an even more difficult time with your appeal. There is no second place in this game called criminal defense, and perhaps that is why you can always have a public defender that will be your advocate.

I interned in the Public Defender's office in my local county during my final year in law school. I learned that Public Defenders are not necessarily attorneys that are less qualified than any other attorney, but they are overworked and underpaid. The amount of time that a public defender is going to spend on a case is marginal at best. They are trained to plea an individual out as quickly as possible, so as to reduce their case load quicker than cases are being assigned to them. This is a race that one cannot win.

The unfortunate aspect about plea bargaining is that the focus is on how good of a deal they can get their client with negotiations with the prosecutor. It never seems to deal with the truth of the accusation. If I am accused of a crime, I want an attorney that will advocate for my innocence, not just a reduction from a five-year sentence to six months in jail. Consider what the scriptures say about the greatest public defender of all time.

Revelation 12:10 says that *"the accuser of our brethren is cast down, which accused them before our God day and night."* The enemy is relentless in bringing accusations about us before the judge, but the back of the Book says that Satan loses the case when we sign on with our defender, Jesus Christ. *"And they overcame him by the blood of the lamb and by the word of their testimony."* (Revelation 12:11). An attorney defending an individual is only as good as the individual is in being open with him. Psalms 5:11 says, *"But let all them that put their trust in thee rejoice: let them shout for joy, because thou defendest them…"*

There are two types of justice. Moral justice and legal justice. Moral justice relates to the decisions that are made as to what is right and what is wrong based on an intrinsic set of values, articulated by the Word of God. Legal justice is demonstrated in the courtrooms all around our country and world. Since God is long suffering, there is often a lag in moral justice and a feeling that moral justice is absent in the majority of society.

In the absence of immediate moral justice, men begin to look to legal justice to make things right. We feel cheated in this area as criminals go free, crime begins to rise and the streets become more and more unsafe. At this point we begin to question how someone who is a Christian could be a public defender even though Christ is the ultimate public defender.

In the absence of immediate moral justice, men begin to look to legal justice to make things right.

In his book, *"The Search for Justice,"* famed defense attorney, Robert Shapiro, explains, "These days an accusation is enough to destroy a life; an indictment and trial holds that life up to the examination and judgment of a society. A defense attorney's job is to see that the man or woman who stands under the scrutiny doesn't stand there alone." This is what the Lord does for us. He insures that we do not face the temptations and trails of life alone. I am glad that heaven has a public defender.

The legal justice system is based on a presumption of innocence. The moral justice system is based on a presumption of guilt. The Bible says in Psalms 51:5, *"Behold, I was shapen in iniquity; and in sin did my mother conceive me."* We have something from the very beginning that is referred to in criminal law as "mens rea" which is Latin for a guilty mind. In a legal justice system, you do not have "mens rea" until you commit a crime. You cannot be convicted of a premeditated crime in a legal justice system unless the prosecutor can prove you have "mens rea," a guilty mind. There is a presumption of innocence.

In a moral justice system, it is just the opposite. The "mens rea" comes built in. It comes with our flesh. Paul says in Romans, *"It (unrighteousness) is imputed to us from Adam."* We have an advocate; a phenomenal public defender that is much more than just a worthy opponent. He operates in the highest court of the universe; the moral justice courtroom. He advocates for us. Paul says in Romans 7 that even though he desired to serve God, there was a law in his body that would war against the law of his mind and bring him into sin. He then concludes in the last verse that even though he has a fleshly nature that wars against righteousness, he can have a free mind to serve the laws of God. God delivers our mind.

In Florida, a person that has been arrested must be brought before a judge within 24 hours for a probable cause hearing. The prosecution must put together their case against the defendant quickly, at least to the point that he or she can establish that they have probable cause sufficient to hold the accused. **The "accuser of the brethren," as the Bible describes Satan, tries to build a case against individuals quickly. This is one reason that children are under attack at such an early age.**

The "accuser of the brethren" is not a comic book figure with a pitch fork and little horns. He is very skilled and very professional. He is not looking for justice, he is looking for vengeance. He is relentless in his attacks. It is not a battle that we can win without our advocate fighting for our defense. We are not smart enough or experienced enough to defend ourselves. The Public Defender is ready to assist, just say the word.

The Bible says in 1 John 2:2, "*He is the propitiation for our sins: and not for ours only, but also for the sins of the whole world.*" The word propitiation is defined as *the act of regaining the favor of. God* puts us back in favor with the moral court of justice. Everyone can afford this lawyer because He does not want your wallet, He wants your heart. He will defend, deliver and preserve, but to get an acquittal, He has to build His case.

Everyone can afford this lawyer because He does not want your wallet, He wants your heart.

Revelation 12:11 says the trial was won by the blood of the Lamb and by the word of their testimony. We have the DNA. We have the blood stains at the scene of the crime. We know that where there used to be sin and sorrow, it has now been stained with the blood of the lamb. The handwritten charges that were against us have been erased with the blood of the Lamb. (Colossians 2:14). We have testimony. We have witnesses. Expert witnesses that testify to the life changing nature of God's love.

The jury comes back with a decision of not guilty. The Public Defender smiles. The defendant leaps for joy and the "accuser of the brethren" storms out of the court room, throws his papers at the law clerk and shouts, "Who's next?"

CHAPTER TWENTY-THREE
The Search for Truth

❖

Wallace Hartley was a violinist that led an ensemble of five accomplished musicians. They had the honor of playing selections from the White Star songbook for the first class passengers on the Titanic. After the collision on that fateful night, they all gathered together in the first class lounge to entertain the passengers, beginning with ragtime and other cheerful numbers. Later they moved to the boat deck foyer, and finally out onto the deck itself.

As women and children entered lifeboats, Major Peuchen heard the band playing "Alexander's Ragtime Band" near boat #6. Harold Bride recalled that the band switched to playing "Song of Autome," a popular tune in the British Dance Halls, as the ship sank further into the sea. The band played cheerful hymns refusing to acknowledge the environment of doom. Lawrence Beesley remembered seeing one of the cello players as late as 12:40 a.m. stabbing the spike of his instrument into a sliding plank on the sinking deck attempting to stabilize his instrument. Edwina Troutt, later described hearing "Nearer My God to Thee" as the ship sank.

Truth does not change with modern times or diminish with passing fads.

Truth is not subject to popular opinion. It is not swayed by music or emotions. Truth does not change with modern times or diminish with passing fads. It stands alone. A sentry on the wall of human order. The truth was that the Titanic was sinking. You could not avoid this truth. You could not decorate this truth with the harmony of accomplished musicians. The fact remained, the ship is sinking and we need a life boat.

There was a professor that taught us in trial law, "If the facts are against you, argue the law, if the law is against you, argue the facts." One student raised his hand and wondered what you do if both are against you. The professor responded,

"Run up your billable hours!" In other words, you will most likely lose so make as much money as you can. I wondered where the search for truth and justice was in all of this. These lofty ideals are lost by the second year of law school. For me the law was more majestic than just a tool to make money, but it could only be as grand as its relationship to truth. Without truth it is only a means to an end.

I can't get away from this little verse in the Bible that just simply says, *"and ye shall know the truth and the truth shall make you free."* (John 8:32). It seems to me that if we desire to be free and to help our clients be free, then truth would be a significant part of this equation. We live in a generation where the value for absolutes has diminished greatly. A generation that considers the contemplation of truth as more important than the knowledge of truth is called postmodernism. A generation of postmodernism is a time when relativism is regarded over revelation.

A generation of postmodernism is a time when relativism is regarded over revelation.

Perhaps it was not intended, but the subjective nature of helping God to establish truth is revealed in the bumper sticker, *"God said it, I believe it, that settles it."* While this sounds like a statement of settled fact, it is more of a subjective agreement. The more accurate statement is *"God said it, that settles it."*

In the book, *The Day America told the Truth*, extensive opinion surveys, where the participants were guaranteed anonymity, were revealed. The results were alarming. Only 13% of America sees all Ten Commandments as binding on us today. 91% of Americans do not tell the truth regularly at home and at work. The survey posed the question, "What would you be willing to do for 10 million dollars?" The answers came back that 25% would abandon their families, 23% would become a prostitute for a week, and 7% would murder a stranger.

I suppose these statistics may reveal that in our post modern society truth is not the centerpiece of our thinking, but I am still idealistic enough to believe that we hunger for truth. In the heart of every man or woman, there is a desire to be free. **We must understand and embrace the fact that freedom is inextricably linked to truth.** Perhaps this journey begins with a pursuit of the "Spirit of truth."

John 14:17 says, *"Even the Spirit of truth; whom the world cannot receive, because it seeth him not, neither knoweth him: but ye know him; for he dwelleth with you, and shall be in you."* If freedom is linked to truth (and it is), and if truth cannot be separated from Christ (and it can't), then truth is a bridge that brings man back to God. The abandonment of truth does more than just destroy our legal system, it destroys our ability to reconcile with our creator.

In law school, we were taught that the best answer was always, "It depends." In reality this is often the correct answer because there are so many variables to every proposition. Beyond the expediency of the answer, is a notion that nothing is set in stone. Early on, we, as law students, wanted to know what the *black letter law* was in each of our studies. The professors never wanted to give us this clear-cut ground to stand on. They would teach us that the law is fluid. It is in flux. It is ever moving and changing. This type of mental bombardment challenges your value system of absolutes.

The Word of God is based on absolutes. If the law is ever changing and moving, then the law parts company, at this point, with the Word of God. The Word of God is based on absolutes. The ministry of Jesus is based on the belief that the words of Christ are embodied in the claim that Jesus made in John 14:6, when he said He was *"The way, the truth and the life."* These absolutes are not restrictive, they are liberating. Any search for truth must begin with a search for the Spirit of truth and the Spirit of truth is part and parcel to the Spirit of God.

In the study of law and in the practice of law, there are two different forms of application for the legal principle. These two forms are called the letter of the law and the spirit of the law. The letter of the law is based on what the statute says on its face. The spirit of the law looks at the intention of the statute and whether or not the intention of the statute was met even though the letter of the statue was not. Courts have ruled in favor of the spirit of the law on many occasions but this does not equate with the search for truth, it only reveals a search for justice. The spirit or essence of a law is what we know is often sufficient to have a correct outcome, but the Spirit of truth is impossible without a Biblical basis.

Article 6 of the U.S. Constitution says "This constitution shall be the supreme law of the land and the judges in every state shall be bound thereby, anything in the constitution or laws of any state to the contrary notwithstanding." In any kind of a conflict between state law and federal law, state law must yield to federal law. It is important to remember this when you consider God's Truth and man's laws. This principle is illustrated in the trial of Jesus.

Pilate, the Roman governor who presided over the trial of Jesus, was wrestling with truth, justice and political expediency as the book of John records in the 18th chapter. Finally, after forsaking the notion of judging on the side of principle and truth, Pilate asked a rhetorical question in verse 38, *"What is truth?"* This was not necessarily a question of curiosity; it was more of a statement concerning his position in this trial. Perhaps Pilate thought: *"No one really knows what the truth of the matter is and even though I do not see the evidence in this case, since I have to make a decision, I choose political expediency. If these Jews don't settle down, it is going to make me look bad back in Rome."*

Pilate mistakenly believed that he had the final authority. He believed that truth was not the critical path in this trial. Jesus let Pilate know that his decision was insignificant in the grand scheme of things because truth will have the final say. Pilate did not see it that way. He saw himself as having the final say. How do you determine what is truth by cross examining absolute Truth? That is like the pig telling the farmer what he wants for breakfast.

I see men with royal robes and pointy pipes sitting around pontificating with an air of superiority about the authority of the scriptures and the relevance of the Gospel. They are attempting to reduce Christianity to the same playing field as secular philosophy; as if our opinion really matters. Just because one has the might does not mean one has the right. Just because one has choices, does not mean one has authority. **Once one leaves absolute truth, personal truth is on a sliding scale of wants and needs.**

Just because one has choices, does not mean one has authority.

I want to make the case that truth is paramount in all that we do. In a day when truth is determined by consensus and justice is determined by a 5 to 4 vote, we need to wrap ourselves in the absolute truth of the Word of God. When Jesus taught, His message was not a multiplicity of ideas and concepts. He did not invite an exchange of popular opinions. He spoke the truth without fear. It all boils down to whether we will conform our life to the Word or attempt fool-heartedly to conform the Word to our life.

Thomas Jefferson feared that America would embrace democracy to the point that the tyranny of the majority would be a reality. His fears may have been justified because **democracy only works when the people that rule are ruled by God.** Truth by itself, and faith in that truth are the underpinnings of our democracy. If truth is losing ground in our courts, it does not have to lose ground in our hearts.

If truth is losing ground in our courts, it does not have to lose ground in our hearts.

Henry Rostun was the captain of the Carpathia. The Carpathia was the ship that rescued 735 passengers, plucking them out of a frigid sea, where the great Titanic once sailed. Crossing a sea littered with the landmines of deadly icebergs, under a pitch dark sky at break neck speeds, the Carpathia arrived in only 90 minutes after the Titanic sank. After the Rescue, Captain Rostun commented, "When day broke, and I looked back at the ice field we had covered under darkness, I shuttered and could only think that some other hand than mine was on the helm that night."

I would rather steer a rescue boat across dangerous waters than just perform pointless music and pretend that there is not a crisis. If we do *something* rather than *nothing*, we may be able to rescue some people along the way.

THE EVIDENCE
The Nature of God to Prove Himself

❖

Evidence can be a two-edged sword. Evidence that proves a positive result like a person's innocence is applauded by all, but evidence that proves guilt or wrongdoing is not welcomed by the guilty party.

I remember as a boy attempting to play football in my home with friends. We broke a lamp and that lamp was evidence that a forbidden activity had been exercised in my parents' absence. My friends and I tried to hide the evidence, but the missing lamp was evidence in and of itself.

Notwithstanding the above example, evidence is not always clear cut. One piece of evidence may point you in one direction and the presentation of that same evidence by another advocate may bring an opposite result. The subjective interpretation of evidence can bring two different people to two different conclusions.

Much is said in law about the restriction of certain types of evidence. Not all evidence is credible. Some evidence has more prejudicial than probative value. **The laws of evidence seek to utilize evidence for the purpose of finding facts rather than for the purpose of distraction and distortion.**

In studying the nature of God, we quickly learn that God is an advocate for accurate evidence. He gives us evidence for many of His blessings, manifestations and higher callings. The evidence of His existence. The evidence of His Word. The evidence of His Spirit. The evidence of His love, His mercy, and many others. We must also know that our enemy, as an angel of light, attempts to create the appearance of evidence for the purpose of distraction.

In this section we will attempt to show the difference and to highlight the indisputable objective evidence that strengthens our faith in God. These truths are made stronger in our hearts and minds by using the laws of evidence to illustrate the solid ground of fact that each believer stands on.

CHAPTER TWENTY-FOUR
The Evidence of His Existence

❖

Evidence is defined as testimony or tangibles offered to prove or disprove the truth of a proposition of fact under investigation or litigation. Every belief requires a certain internal investigation where we put the evidence or lack thereof under the microscope of human credibility.

The Word of God begins with the simple statement, *"In the beginning, God created the heaven and the earth."* This statement brings two propositions into the realm of question. The first is that God does not have a beginning. He has always existed. Creation has a beginning, but God does not. The second proposition is that God created what we see and enjoy. The first proposition offers evidence of a testimony, and the second proposition offers tangible evidence. One speaks to the visible and the other speaks to the invisible, yet both offer evidence.

Testimonial evidence is a witness' spoken report of a happening or circumstance observed by the witness. This evidence can be either direct or circumstantial. Tangible evidence is a person or thing which is itself direct or circumstantial evidence of the material proposition of fact. The testimony of God's existence speaks to direct evidence. Direct evidence is evidence that speaks directly to the truth or falsity of fact under investigation or litigation.

When God through His spoken Word testifies that He was in the beginning, He is testifying as a direct eye witness of fact. He was there. He was the only one there. He testifies to the fact directly.

Direct evidence is in contrast to circumstantial evidence that speaks indirectly to a material proposition by asserting some other proposition of fact from which a logical mind may draw the conclusion of inference.

Direct evidence would be a witness testifying that he saw the building on fire. Circumstantial evidence would be a witness testifying that he saw smoke coming out of the building and believed it to be on fire. The circumstantial evidence requires the inference that where there is smoke, there must be fire.

Circumstantial evidence is less substantive. The smoke may have been coming from a different source. It may have been from a fireplace, a smoke machine, a cigar or a stove. To eliminate the other options additional evidence or testimony must be presented to substantiate the circumstantial evidence.

Any proposition of fact that suggests any other evidence of the existence of God at the beginning can only be circumstantial. No other witness can testify directly to the non-existence of God. Any other evidence requires inference. It is only circumstantial at best and less reliable. An atheist has a more difficult, less reliable task of proving a non-existent God.

In His book, *What's so Great about Christianity*, author Dinesh D'Souza states, "Scientists call the starting moment of the universe a singularity, an original point at which neither space nor time nor scientific laws are in effect. Nothing can be known scientifically about what came before such a point. Indeed the term *before* has no meaning since time itself did not exist prior to the singularity."

The singularity points to the fact that there is only one eye witness and He has testified with direct evidence. One must then conclude that any evidence to the contrary is less reliable despite the testimony of an invisible God. The enemy will attempt to use the visible (science) to trump the invisible (God), but falls short of credibility in the laws of evidence.

God has a self-proving nature that continues to build an indisputable case.

Everything about God is evidential. God has a self-proving nature that continues to build an indisputable case. The tangible evidence of God's creation makes the case even stronger. We can see the earth and even parts of the heaven. This tangible evidence takes root in our logic. The scripture confirms this notion with the statement in Psalms 14:1, *"The fool hath said in his heart, There is no God."*

The only way to challenge this tangible evidence is to attempt to offer evidence that is more prejudicial than probative. If we serve a God that has created this earth that we live on, and the heavens that we stand in wonder of, then we are accountable to Him for our actions. This accountability goes against the grain of our flesh. Thus, if some other evidence could attempt to show a different origin, humanity is ready for such a proposition regardless of the likelihood or probative value.

This is where the "Big Bang" theory and the "Origin of Species" theory have their roots. Remember that we said in the outset of this chapter, that our opposition will also offer evidence. In a court of law such evidence designed to appeal to our nature rather than advance the search for truth would not be allowed. The rules of evidence would require greater substantive value.

Tangible evidence is sometimes further subdivided into real evidence and demonstrative evidence. Real evidence is a person or thing which is itself direct or circumstantial evidence of a material fact. Demonstrative evidence is not evidence at all, but is commonly spoken of as if it were. It is, in reality, merely a visual or audiovisual demonstration or illustration of testimonial evidence. In the absence of such underlying testimonial evidence, demonstrative evidence has no probative value at all.

Creation speaks for itself. The earth declares its origin by its very existence. Creation for the purposes of tangible evidence is real. It is direct evidence of a material fact. For humanity to attempt to prove otherwise is to provide demonstrative evidence without the underlying testimonial evidence. This is not evidence at all and has no probative value.

Creation speaks for itself. The earth declares its origin by its very existence.

The eternal existence of God as the creator is the most reliable evidence that we have. It not only substantiates the beginning of this world that we are part of, it also reveals that God provides evidence that is indisputable. It shouts loud and clear from the very beginning that God is a giver of truth based on His laws and our laws.

CHAPTER TWENTY-FIVE
Judicial Notice

❖

There are certain things in life as well as the law that are without dispute. We know the sun provides light and heat for the earth. We know there is a difference between a male and a female. We know there will come a time when the body will wear out and die. These are well recognized facts that everyone knows. They are not facts under dispute.

The law has a vehicle of judicial expediency that allows certain statements or facts to be stipulated to and not contested. Facts that are stipulated to are facts that both sides agree to that are not a part of the controversy. Judicial Notice is a vehicle that the courts use to expedite the process of judgment with well established facts.

Judicial Notice simply means: "the decision by a court recognizing the validity of certain facts without the need for proof, thereby relieving one party of the burden of producing evidence to prove the facts." An example of Judicial Notice would be the address that a defendant lives at or where certain parties work.

If a fact is established by the court as Judicial Notice, then evidence is not needed to prove it.

If a fact is established by the court as Judicial Notice, then evidence is not needed to prove it. The judge recognizes the fact is proven because of guarantees of accuracy and certainty outside the processes of the courtroom. This allows the court to focus on the issues that are under dispute and that do need evidence.

The Bible tells us that we have an adversary that is *"an accuser of the brethren"* in Revelation 12:10. The adversary is attempting to build a case against us that will keep us out of heaven. The good news is that the Bible reminds us in I John 2:1 that we have an advocate or an attorney named Jesus Christ that is representing us. This is a struggle of epic proportions, but there are some facts that both sides have stipulated to without controversy.

Consider some well established facts that have guarantees of accuracy outside of human opinion. James 2:9 says, *"Thou believest that there is one God, thou doest well: the devils also believe and tremble."* Isaiah 43:11 says, *"I, even I, am the Lord, and beside me there is no savior."* Both sides have stipulated to the fact that there is only one God. It is not under dispute.

Consider this judicial notice in the spirit world. Acts 4:12 says *"Neither is there salvation in any other: for there is none other name under heaven given among men, whereby we must be saved."* Luke 10:17 says *"..Lord, even the devils are subject unto us through thy name."*

The scripture confirms that both sides have stipulated to the fact that there is a God, there is only one God and His name is Jesus. This could only be established because of guarantees of accuracies outside of God's courtroom. Every time the sun rises, every time an earnest prayer is prayed to a false god and it returns void, every time someone is healed in the name of Jesus, the guarantees of accuracy are further established.

In a civil trial the jury must accept the Judicial Notice as a fact, but in a criminal case, the jury **may** accept the Judicial Notice as fact. We are the jury. We can accept the Judicial Notice as fact or fiction, but the counselors in God's court have already moved beyond those undisputed facts.

Evidence is a peculiar tool. To the mother of a defendant, there will never be enough evidence to convince her that it was her son that "did it." To the mother of the victim perhaps there will never be enough evidence to exonerate the defendant.

Evidence may never be strong enough to override the paradigm of emotional persuasion, but God uses evidence to persuade the fence sitters and perhaps even some naysayers. God knows that a man's heart is not always on the same page as his mind. We know some things in our heart that we may not want to consent to with our minds. God uses evidence on this battlefield to answer questions that man cannot. Perhaps we should call it "Spiritual Notice."

God knows that a man's heart is not always on the same page as his mind.

CHAPTER TWENTY-SIX
Relevancy

❖

Hebrews 4:12 contains an interesting description of the Word of God. It states *"the Word of God is **quick**, and powerful, and sharper than any two edged sword."* The word "quick" here denotes living, adaptable, and relevant.

The Barnes Commentary says, "It (the Word of God) is not dead, inert, and powerless. It has a living power, and is energetic and active. It is *adapted* to produce this effect." The Geneva Commentary says, "the Word of God is living, because of the effect it has on those to whom it is preached."

The Word of God is not an ancient book that is unrealistic and irrelevant in our lives today.

The Word of God is not an ancient book that is unrealistic and irrelevant in our lives today. It is applicable to each area of our life. To describe this aspect of the Word of God, we describe it as living and breathing. It would have to be relevant to be applicable and admissible.

Imagine that every life is a trial. Your life and my life. Each of us are presenting evidence to our mind and to our emotions of what decisions we should make, and what value choices we should make. Every day these decisions are made based on the evidence that we determine is credible and relevant. If the Word of God is going to be a crucial part in the decision making process, then it should be relevant.

In a court of law, the beginning of any analysis as to what evidence is inadmissible and what is, is to determine the relevancy. **Relevance is the relationship between an item of evidence and a fact (or proposition) which that item of evidence is intended to prove.** For evidence to be allowed in a court of law, there must be relevance. The proposed evidence has to pertain to what is being debated, and what the issue in the case is.

If something is going to dictate the steps of our life, it should be relevant to our life. The Word of God is relevant to guide our steps and to direct our paths. It contains the original moral code. It gives the rule of law and then makes it applicable by example and instruction. It even amended the rule of law with additional clarification and guidance in the New Testament.

We consider the necessary evidence that is needed to determine truth in our life. All evidence must begin with the Bible. We consider the relevance of the relationship between an item of evidence (the Bible) and the fact or proposition (the right choices) which that item of evidence is intended to prove. It is clear that not only should the Word of God be allowed as relevant, but it is the centerpiece of our evidence.

On the other hand consider evidence that is not relevant. It does not matter to me what a movie star thinks about who I should vote for, or what kind of a car I should drive or whether or not I should be faithful to my wife. It is simply not relevant. Their direction should not be a factor in this trial called my life because it is not relevant.

It seems curious that we listen to them and allow our emotions to accept their opinions into our decision making process. One should not get moral direction from Hollywood. If we looked at it strictly from the stand point of the relevancy of the evidence, any court would not allow it. **Federal Rules of Evidence 403 states: "Relevant evidence may be excluded if its probative value is substantially outweighed by the danger of: Unfair Prejudice, Confusion of the issues, Misleading the Jury and Waste of Time."**

Clearly these tactics by a secular society is not anything new. The distraction and confusion somehow creates a distorted sense of what is reliable and what is not when we consider the important questions in life concerning our values and choices.

Once when I was teaching a Home Bible Study to a young family, I read from scripture concerning the biblical account of the Children of Israel crossing the Red Sea. One of the participants took issue with the legitimacy of the biblical account. He exclaimed, "I don't believe it happened that way in real life. I saw the movie, *The Ten Commandments*, and it happened differently." To this man, the movie was a more reliable source of truth than the Holy Scriptures.

CHAPTER TWENTY-SEVEN
Evidence In an Earthen Vessel

❖

In Jeremiah 32, we read an interesting story about the prophet Jeremiah buying some land under God's instruction. Jeremiah 32:10 describes the prophet subscribing the evidence and sealing it with witnesses. Jeremiah 32:11 says the evidence was both sealed and open. The next verse states that Jeremiah took the evidence of the purchase according to the law and customs and gave it to the witnesses. He then charged these witnesses to put the evidence in earthen vessels (Jeremiah 32:14).

God gives us evidence of what He is doing in our life.

In this passage of scripture, the Lord was instructing Jeremiah to follow the letter of the law concerning the purchase of this property that Jeremiah had a legal right to redeem. The Lord knew that if the evidences were not carefully followed, there could be a challenge to the owner of the property at a future date. This passage also illustrates how God gives us evidence of what He is doing in our life.

In Jeremiah 32:10, the evidence was written and sealed with witnesses. God uses His Word to build an indisputable case. He uses witnesses and evidence. God gave Noah a visible sign of the promise to never destroy the earth again by water. It was a rainbow. God gave Abraham a visible sign of His promise to make him a great nation. It was a son in his old age. II Corinthians 13:1 declares, *"In the mouth of two or three witnesses, shall every word be established."* It appears that God understands and uses the weight of evidence.

The story is even more interesting when you consider that the scripture says some of the evidence was sealed and some was open. The scripture says twice that the Prophet instructed the witness to take both the open evidence and the sealed evidence and put it in an earthen vessel for the sake of preservation.

It would not seem like an earthen vessel or a vessel of clay would preserve the evidence. Yet, the Dead Sea Scrolls were found in such vessels after nearly 1800 years. These scrolls in their original form are on display in Jerusalem today, and one can see how these shaky vessels of clay preserved the scrolls.

II Corinthians 4:7 says; *"But we have this treasure in earthen vessels that the excellency of the power may be of God, and not of us."* The text goes on to describe this treasure as an internal strength that keeps us from being distressed though troubled on every side, from feeling forsaken though persecuted and from being destroyed though cast down.

God is continuing this same process of putting evidence in earthen vessels. Evidence that is a treasure. **There are two issues to consider, what is the earthen vessel and what is the treasure?** We cannot study one without both being revealed. If we consider the fact that we are vessels of clay or vessels from the earth by the mere fact that we are created from the dust of the earth, it seems clear that the Word is pointing us to the fact that we as humans are the earthen vessels, but let us examine more scripture.

God is continuing this same process of putting evidence in earthen vessels.

Jeremiah 32:44 states, *"Men shall buy fields for money and subscribe evidences, and seal them, and take witnesses."* Perhaps this subscribed evidence is similar to what we think of today when we get a receipt. It is a piece of paper that is evidence of our purchase.

II Corinthians 3:2-3 states, *"Ye are our epistle written in our hearts, known and read of all men: Forasmuch as ye are manifestly declared to be the epistle of Christ ministered by us, written not with ink, but with the Spirit of the living God; not in tables of stone, but in fleshy tables of the heart."* This scripture text reveals the container and the treasure.

We are earthen vessels. We are made from the dust of the earth. We are just flesh and bones on our own, but with God's Spirit in our life we become containers of a treasure unlike anything the world has ever known. Our life is written evidence that Christ has redeemed us or purchased us through His blood.

The Spirit of God is the treasure. It is the evidence that has been put in the containers of human life. The book of Jeremiah reminds us that the evidence is both sealed and revealed, internal and external, visible and invisible.

In the book of Jeremiah, the Lord wanted the prophet to follow the letter of the law in buying the land because even if the land is destroyed and the people taken captive, there will be evidence of the purchase. If there is evidence, then the day will come when the heirs of Jeremiah will be able to redeem the promise even in the midst of adversity.

God has put evidence of His glory and His power in us.

The evidence that the Lord has given us is able to be redeemed at a later date. Even in the face of adversity as severe as death, the treasure in earthen vessels will be visible evidence. The Bible says in Romans 8:11, *"But if the Spirit of him that raised up Jesus from the dead dwell in you, he that raised up Christ from the dead shall also quicken your mortal bodies by his Spirit that dwelleth in you."*

This evidence has already been established. In the courts of heaven it has already been decided. The evidence though visible and invisible, though sealed and revealed is preserved unto that day. It has been placed in a vulnerable, yet durable, vessel called humanity.

CHAPTER TWENTY-EIGHT
Not Admissible

❖

When my young twin sons, Gregory and Luke, were not able to read or write, they would try to pick out a word or two that they recognized while my wife or I read to them. However, this did not deter them from finding ways to communicate in written form.

During this time, the twins found a white piece of thin cardboard that was left over from a discarded toy package. They tore off a portion of it and pushed a hole through it so the cardboard could hang on their door knob to their room. They found a pen and wrote the word, "*NO*," and hung it on their door knob. When my wife and I inquired as to what this was all about, they informed us that when the sign is on their door, they were busy and no one was allowed in their room. I thought seriously about hanging the sign on our door.

Most evidence is not allowed into court. Before a trial begins there are many pre-trial motions that will ask the court to not allow certain evidence to be used in trial. A motion to suppress evidence will ask the court to disallow certain evidence based on the manner in which the evidence was obtained. This is often referred to as "fruit from the poisonous tree."

If evidence was obtained through an illegal search, then that evidence will be thrown out even though it may be very good evidence. The idea behind this is that everything that flows from an illegal search is illegal in and of itself. If the root is rotten, then everything that hangs on the tree is rotten. If testimony was obtained through inappropriate coercion then, even though you may have a confession, it would not be allowed in court.

If the root is rotten, then everything that hangs on the tree is rotten.

The enemy of our soul is always trying to get evidence on the record against us. The Bible describes the enemy of our soul as *"the accuser of the brethren."* (Revelation 12:10). The accuser has many illegal tactics that he uses to try and get evidence against us. He will then try to use this evidence to convict us. Satan is a constant accuser. He is a relentless prosecutor of believers. The good news is that our attorney is also the judge, and He will not allow inappropraite evidence to be used in the case against us.

Romans 8:33 and 34 says, *"Who shall lay any thing to the charge of God's elect? It is God that justifieth. Who is he that condemneth? It is Christ that died, yea rather, that is risen again, who is even at the right hand of God, who also maketh intercession for us."* God will not allow evidence to be used against us that is illegal. The accuser does not have legal right to bring charges against us based on an illegal origin. When Satan tries to convict us and condemn us, we must remind him that his evidence is inadmissible.

The Federal Rules of Evidence 404(a) says, "Pass or prior bad acts are not admissible to prove Character." Legally we assume that people rehabilitate themselves after a bad act and therefore do not allow that bad act into evidence unless under certain circumstances. To show someone did something 99 times isn't admissible to show they did it again on the 100th time.

The Devil can't bring up our past.

Character, as a general element of a case, is not admissible for the purpose of proving that the defendant acted in conformity therewith on a particular occasion. The Devil can't bring up our past. That won't stop him from trying, but it is not allowed unless the defendant introduces his own character. If he does, then it is free game for the prosecution. This is called the "open door" rule. If we are going to keep bringing our past up, our opponent will too and he will jump on it, and pound us with it like a sledge hammer.

Isaiah 3:9 says, *"The show of their countenance doth witness against them; and they declare their sin as Sodom, they hide it not. Woe unto their soul! for they have rewarded evil unto themselves."* If we are going to bring up our sins and allow it to be a part of our present record, then the accuser is going have a legal right to use the same testimony against us. **If we introduce it, then we can't claim inadmissibility.** If we struggled in our past and did some things that we are not proud of, we need to ask God to forgive us and then forgive ourselves. After that, leave it alone. Don't talk about it. Don't brag about it. Let it die!

The Federal Rules of Evidence Rule 407 prohibits the admission of subsequent remedial measures when the evidence is offered to prove negligence or culpable conduct. If we fix something, it cannot be used to prove that it was broken. The law recognizes that if we are trying to make things right, those good acts cannot be admitted into court to show that our actions were an admission of wrong doing. This is a public policy issue to encourage people to make things right.

The "accuser of the brethren" tried to bring up the fact that Paul was a killer of Christians before he was saved, but the Lord responded, "not admissible." When the accuser tried to bring up the fact that Peter denied the Lord before he received the Holy Ghost, the Lord responded, "not admissible." When accusers brought the lady caught in adultery (John 8:4) to Jesus for judgment, the Lord said, "not admissible."

In Romans 8:35, the rhetorical question is asked, *"Who shall separate us from the love of Christ? shall tribulation, or distress, or persecution, or famine, or nakedness, or peril, or sword?"* The answer comes back loud and strong in verses 37-39, *"Nay, in all these things we are more than conquerors through him that loved us. For I am persuaded, that neither death, nor life, nor angels, nor principalities, nor powers, nor things present, nor things to come, Nor height, nor depth, nor any other creature, shall be able to separate us from the love of God, which is in Christ Jesus our Lord."* Nothing can stop us from coming to Christ and growing in Christ. All the evidence has been thrown out.

What inadmissible evidence has the accuser tried to use against you as an individual? Has he tried to destroy your life with your past? Has he tried to convince your mind that it is impossible to remediate the prior bad acts in your life? Has the accuser attempted to use your own thoughts as the jury and convict you with inadmissible and inappropriate evidence? Perhaps you should just hang a "NO" sign on the door of your heart and your mind. Go forward in the grace and knowledge that your heavenly judge has acquitted you. Celebrate the freedom of a clear conscience.

Celebrate the freedom of a clear conscience.

CHAPTER TWENTY-NINE
Hearsay

❖

Hearsay is oral or written testimony made out of court and offered to prove the truth of the matter asserted. It is normally reported by someone other than the author of the assertion, and thereby less reliable. In other words, it is second hand conversation or communication. Hearsay by definition is not admissible into evidence. There are so many exceptions to the traditional hearsay rule that often the exceptions swallow the rule. However, these exceptions bring other indicators of credibility so that the evidence is admissible. One exception of interest is excited utterance. **The Federal Rules of Evidence 803(2) state that excited utterance is "a statement relating to a startling event or condition made while the declarant was under the stress of excitement caused by the event or condition."**

This external evidence gave witness to the power and legitimacy of God pouring out His Spirit on humanity.

Excited utterances are deemed trustworthy because they are made so quickly and reflexively that we have some confidence that the declarant had no opportunity to shape them to his own self interest or other ulterior motive. Excited utterances are admissible because they are the source of evidence closest in time to the events reported and least subject to the recreative reflection to which in court testimony is vulnerable.

In Acts 1:8, the Lord promises His followers power and strength in the face of discouragement with these words of comfort, *"But ye shall receive power, after that the Holy Ghost is come upon you: and ye shall be witnesses unto me.."* God is going to give witness to this covenant or contract of the Holy Spirit being given to mankind. It will be sealed and it will be visible. It will have witnesses and it will have evidence. What kind of evidence do we have of the Holy Spirit or Holy Ghost that is visible?

Acts 2:4 states, *"And they were all filled with the Holy Ghost, and begin to speak with other tongues, as the Spirit gave them utterance."* This utterance was driven by the Spirit and was a visible sign of God's covenant to pour out His Spirit. Acts 2:6 says, *"Every man heard them speak in his own language."* These witnesses were from different countries and were amazed to hear these Galileans speak in their native language. In Acts 2:8, this reaction is recorded, *"And how hear we every man in our own tongue, wherein we were born?"*

This utterance was visible evidence of a treasure in earthen vessels and was witnessed by many. Something externally demonstrated what God was doing internally. This external evidence gave witness to the power and legitimacy of God pouring out His Spirit on humanity.

In Acts 10, the same spiritual infilling occurs when Cornelius receives the promise. Acts 10:45-46 explains that there were witnesses and a visible sign. *"And they of the circumcision which believed were astonished, as many as came with Peter, because that on the Gentiles also was poured out the gift of the Holy Ghost. For they heard them speak with tongues, and magnify God."*

The Bible describes this visible evidence of speaking in tongues as utterance given by the Spirit. It appears that the Holy Spirit is given to humanity with evidences that are credible and trustworthy. The human spirit responds with excitement when the Holy Spirit takes up residence in the earthen vessel. This excited utterance is witnessed by the recipient and others that may be nearby.

The human spirit responds with excitement when the Holy Spirit takes up residence in the earthen vessel.

This utterance is the outward evidence that is witnessed and recorded not just in the heart of a man or woman, but also in the ear of a listener. This evidence is not just more reliable by legal principles; it is also part and parcel to the nature of God to give evidence of a covenant that He has made with mankind.

In law school, we were always taught that the judge decides the law and the jury decides the facts. If God is the Judge, and we are the jury, then we cannot change the law. The moral law given to us from the Ten Commandments is established. They can take it out of every classroom and every courtroom in America, but the Law will remain the Law. The jury cannot determine the law, but the jury can decide whether the evidence is sufficient to collaborate the proposition.

We are the jury and we decide the weight and the strength of the evidence God provides. The most persuasive of all evidence is demonstrative evidence. Demonstrative evidence is tangible evidence used for explanatory or illustrative purposes only. The utterance of the Spirit is demonstrative and it is convincing. It is also further proof that God uses evidence in the natural world as well as the spiritual world. God is not foreign to the concept of reliable evidence. God was the creator of evidence, visible and invisible.

CHAPTER THIRTY
Invisible Evidence

❖

I was at a dinner party with some friends, and we were talking about the space program among other events in the news. One of the dinner guests sucked all of the air out of the room when he announced that he did not believe we ever landed on the moon. That statement had everyone's attention. He continued by saying he believed the entire Apollo space program was all shot in a stage studio under a cover of secrecy to convince the world we had passed the Russians in our pursuit of space exploration.1

We questioned his logic for several minutes, and he justified his position by stating he did not believe that we had the technology fifty years ago to land on the moon. One of our friends who used to work for NASA (National Aeronautics and Space Administration) asked him, "Do you believe in satellites?"

Our suspicious friend answered in the affirmative and added, "GPS (Global Positional Satellites) proves that we have satellites in space."

"Well," the NASA friend countered, "satellites have taken pictures of the moon with the lunar lander still sitting there."

The lunar lander is a common term used to describe the Apollo Lunar Module which was a piece of equipment on the Saturn V rockets that allowed the astronauts to descend to the surface of the moon and to ascend back into orbit after the mission on the moon was completed. A portion of the Lunar Module always stayed on the moon and served as a platform for the Module to blast off back into orbit for its return to earth.

I thought our NASA friend had presented irrefutable logic, but our non-believing friend was not convinced. He rebutted, "Well, I have Photo Shop®, too," implying that the photos from the satellites were distorted.

We, by nature live in an invisible world. We gravitate to visible evidence. If we can see it, we believe it. If we cannot see it, we don't believe it and sometimes even if we can see it, we don't believe it. The power to believe is one of the most powerful resources that we have in our humanity. In fact, it is more powerful than the power to love. It will cause us to lay our life down. It will cause us to change our lifestyle. It is the foundation of faith.

The power to believe is one of the most powerful resources that we have in our humanity.

The power to believe is an integral part of being a Christian. In fact we often say, "I'm a believer." When we confess that we believe, we are admitting that we understand and accept invisible evidence. Faith is the ability to see invisible evidence as proof that is just as strong, or perhaps even stronger, in our minds as visible evidence.

Hebrews 11:1 says, *"Now faith is the substance of things hoped for, the evidence of things not seen."* The power to believe is to have such a confidence in what we cannot see that it becomes evidence to our soul. Faith is not pie in the sky, it is substantive. Faith is a part of who we are at our core. We use faith every day in small decisions and big decisions that we may not think twice about. Every time we sit on a chair or ride an elevator, we use faith. We believe in something we did not make, and in the person or persons who made it; even though we may have never seen or met them.

The power to believe is to have such a confidence in what we cannot see that it becomes evidence to our soul.

The power to believe is invisible, but when this power connects with an invisible God it creates such a solid bond of validity that lives are transformed and changed. The social order of our human race is strengthened and more harmonious. The person who is not a believer has not taken the safer route. They are not more secure by refraining from believing in invisible evidence. The reason that faith is so valid is because God uses invisible evidence to connect with an invisible power in us to join us together.

Most evidence that is inadmissible in a trial is not inadmissible because it is visible or invisible; it is inadmissible because the validity of the evidence cannot be tested. Evidence has to be able to be scrutinized so that we are able to determine its truthfulness. The danger of evidence that is more visible than truthful will often prejudice a jury so that the visible nature of the evidence overrides the need to determine the veracity of the evidence.

The Federal Rules of Evidence 403 were created to protect us from ourselves. The rule states, "evidence may be excluded if its probative value is substantially outweighed by the danger of unfair prejudice, confusion of the issues, or misleading the jury, or by considerations of undue delay, waste of time, or needless presentation of cumulative evidence." All of these abuses of evidence are very visible to the point that we forget that it may not be evidence at all. **Rule 403 limits the abuses of evidence that is more visible than valid.**

Hebrews 11:3 continues by saying, *"Through faith we understand that the worlds were framed by the Word of God, so that things which are seen were not made of things which do appear."* In this scripture we see that the creation of visible things, like the earth, is done by invisible things, like the spoken Word of God. This is not necessarily accomplished so that the visible will prove the invisible, but rather that the truth of the invisible evidence will be revealed in the truth of the visible evidence.

We are mortal beings and our nature does not always pick up on the script running behind the picture, so God gives us a truth finder called faith to "flesh out" the invisible evidence. In the Old Testament, the Children of Israel were always battling the temptation to build idols that they could worship. They wanted something visible to look at even though it was built on a lie. God resisted the children of Israel from doing this, and when they disobeyed His Word, there was a removal of God's favor on their lives.

God gives us a truth finder called faith to "flesh out" the invisible evidence.

Leviticus 26:1 says, *"Ye shall make you no idols nor graven image, neither rear you up a standing image, neither shall ye set up any image of stone in your land, to bow down unto it: for I am the LORD your God."* God wanted the Children of Israel to see the invisible evidence. The image of God was not yet revealed. The truth was in the invisible. God gave them His presence, but it is in our nature to want a visible representation of God's power. Moses was used of God as their leader because he could see the invisible God. (Hebrews 11:27).

Have you ever wondered why Satan attacks the family so much? Satan does not attack the family because he wants to mess up our family portraits. He attacks the family because it is the visible image on this earth of an invisible order. In the New Testament, Christ refers to how He is the husband and the church is the bride. This example is given over and over, and quoted during marriage ceremonies. We are to love our wives as Christ loves the church and wives are to honor their husbands as the church honors Christ.

This order breaks down when a third party presents themselves at work or at the gym or wherever, and claims that they love someone more than their spouse or they claim they admire and respect someone more than their spouse. If we believe this false report, we may act upon it and break the bonds of our marriage covenant. This disruption in the family disrupts the covenant that Christ has with the church. That is what Satan did in the Garden of Eden.

Marriage symbolizes an order that is necessary for Christ to be in harmony with the church. It does not stop there. When we forsake invisible evidence for visible evidence, we disrupt the power of faith to keep us in harmony with God.

Paul expanded on this subject in the first chapter of Romans he wrote, *"The invisible things of Him from the creation of the world are clearly seen, being understood by the things that are made, even his eternal power and Godhead; so that they are without excuse."* (Romans 1:20) The same spirit in the Old Testament that erupted when the people left the worship of an invisible God for a visible God is present today when we forsake our faith in God. It is a spirit because it is a clear tactic of the enemy to introduce himself as a third party to disrupt the order of God.

Paul continued in Romans 1:23 explaining what happens when this invisible evidence is lost; *"And changed the glory of the uncorruptible God into an image made like to corruptible man, and to birds, and fourfooted beasts, and creeping things"* He then concluded in the 25th verse, *"Who changed the truth of God into a lie, and worshipped and served the creature more than the Creator, who is blessed forever. Amen."* The result of giving the invisible evidence an image is the lost of the supernatural order of God. This change has drastic results for humanity.

Only God can give the invisible evidence an image. For the invisible God, we receive the image of Jesus. Paul stated in Colossians 1:15-16, that Christ was *"...the image of the invisible God, the firstborn of every creature: For by him were all things created, that are in heaven, and that are in earth, visible and invisible, whether they be thrones, or dominions, or principalities, or powers: all things were created by him, and for him."*

That is why the name of Jesus is fought so hard in the world we live in. It is the expressed image of God. If Satan can mitigate God's image of the invisible, then he can convince us of a substitute, thus getting us to substitute God's image for our image. Invisible evidence for visible evidence. As long as we cleave to God's image, we will not create a false image and open our self up to unclean spirits.

The promise of a rapture when we will be caught away and be with the Lord is invisible evidence. This event, outside of Christ, has not taken place for the natural eye to observe. We just believe. The forgiving power of God is invisible much like electricity, but the image of that forgiveness is illustrated in Calvary. That is why the Bible says He was the Lamb slain from the foundation of the world. Calvary was the image of a loving God that forgives all of our sins. It was the image of invisible evidence. Faith is the evidence of things not seen. And faith can never be taken from us unless we willingly give it up by replacing it with a false image.

Many years ago, I took a group of people to Israel. We had a tour guide named Amos. Amos was well educated and very cynical. He was humored by how much we enjoyed the Holy Land sites. He teased me playfully about my faith. Amos was agnostic, but I believed he was also hungry to know God. We went to the garden tomb area where Jesus was buried, and I was able to go into the empty tomb where there is a sign that says, "He is not here, He is risen." I was rejoicing when I returned to the van and Amos asked me, "How can you be so excited about seeing where He is not?" The Lord helped me to have a quick answer. I said, "Because His absence in the tomb confirms His presence in my heart."

His absence in the tomb confirms His presence in my heart.

CHAPTER THIRTY-ONE
The Rule of Completeness

❖

The story is told of three friends from the local congregation who were asked "When you're in your casket, and friends, family, and congregation members are mourning over you, what would you like them to say?" Artie one of the friends said: "I would like them to say I was a wonderful husband, a fine spiritual leader, and a great family man." Eugene, the second friend commented: "I would like them to say I was a wonderful teacher and servant of God who made a huge difference in people's lives." Don, the third friend shrugged and said: "I'd like them to say, *look, he's moving!*"

Romans 6:6-7 says, *"Knowing this, that our old man is crucified with him, that the body of sin might be destroyed, that henceforth we should not serve sin. For he that is dead is freed from sin."* Body of sin means the whole record. Everything. The wonderful thing about salvation is that it is complete. There is nothing partial about God. He is the whole package. He can completely heal you. He can completely forgive you. He can completely save you. He can completely raise you up. He can turn the still into life. He can turn morning into dancing. He can turn every aspect of your life.

The Rule of Completeness comes from the Federal Rules of Evidence Rule 106. It deals with questions of timing for writings and other kinds of recordings. The rule states, "When a writing or recorded statement or part thereof is introduced by a party, an adverse party may require the introduction at that time of any other part or any other writing or recorded statement which ought in fairness to be considered contemporaneously with it."

If an opponent is only going to offer part of a writing or a recording into evidence against you, Rule 106 allows you to require that the complete written document or recording be submitted into evidence at that time. We cannot take the part that makes our opponent look guilty and leave out the part that exonerates him/her. The evidence must be complete so that the statements can be considered in the proper context.

Anyone of us can point to certain times and certain events when our actions were less than stellar, but God will not allow isolated charges to be used against us. The totality of the circumstances reveals that we have a heart for God and a desire to please him. God's rule of completeness requires that the entire record be considered. The complete record of our lives should include the overwhelming effect that Calvary has on our sins. The complete nature of God gives us complete deliverance and complete forgiveness.

The complete nature of God gives us complete deliverance and complete forgiveness.

Evidence by its very nature has an accumulation effect. Evidence presented systematically and succinctly has the ability to gather steam to the point that is becomes undeniable. Money can accumulate, or more accurately, evaporate very quickly. Judgment accumulates as the Bible describes in the stories of Noah and Lot. Sin can accumulate to the point that it becomes unbearable. Faith accumulates to the point that anything is possible. Regardless of what evidence is built against us, there is nothing more complete, more thorough, or more powerful than the accumulative effect of God's grace.

The Bible tells us in Acts 10 that there was a Roman Centurion who was a just man; who gave to the poor and was prayerful on a consistent basis. His name was Cornelius, and he was sent an angel to give him direction as well as the Apostle Peter to tell him about Jesus. The Bible says that Cornelius' giving contributions and prayers had come up before the Lord as a memorial. (Acts 10:4) These acts of kindness and obedience came up before the Lord as a memorial. An accumulative mountain of evidence was presented in the courtroom of heaven.

Evidence by its very nature has an accumulation effect.

Cornelius was not a Jew. He was not a follower of the ministry of Jesus as far as we can tell from scripture, but he had such a day-by-day consistent desire of God, that the account of his pursuit of God was too big of a mountain to ignore. Every step we take toward God is noted. There is not one prayer or one trip to church that goes unnoticed in heaven. When the enemy comes in and tries to beat us up with a mistake we made, we remind him that he needs to look at the complete record. God does, and He is the one that determines the weight of the evidence.

THE PROPERTY
The Tangible Promises of God

❖

In July of 1999, I had the honorable privilege to study under the Chief Justice of the U.S. Supreme Court, William Rehnquist. We studied at McGill University in Montreal, Canada. The Chief Justice had just completed preceding over the impeachment trial of President William Jefferson Clinton in Washington D.C. President Clinton was acquitted, and the Chief Justice was glad to be on summer vacation and away from Washington D.C.

On the first day of class, this fragile 75-year-old man ambled into class with the dignity of a Disney World® tourist. He had on casual clothes and a straw hat with the name "Tulane" on the brim. His body was bent over and tired, but his mind was razor sharp. He had a bottle of spring water on the table that he drank from occasionally as he altered between sitting down and standing up. This repositioning, he explained, was the result of some recent back discomfort he was experiencing.

I was struck by the fact that this man, though frail and gentile like a granddad, was arguably the most powerful man in the United States as the Chief Justice of the United States Supreme Court on a lifetime appointment. For 48 years he had played a vital role in shaping our laws having first arrived at the Supreme Court as a 27-year-old law clerk. Our archaic laws in property are similar in the fact that they are ancient and seemingly easy to pierce, but do not be deceived, they are very powerful. Our property laws are well worn with time and deeply rooted in the foundation of our national treasure; the right to own property.

Property law is from the common law and common law comes from the Anglo Saxon laws of Europe. Many of the Anglo Saxon laws come from scripture. This was not something that I was aware of until I started studying property laws. Much of the laws in property are like the Old Testament in that they are overlooked and skipped over. Many of them read like Egyptian hieroglyphics and are not very appealing at first glance. However, there are many treasures and nuggets of truth that are hidden in the pages of ancient text if you take a moment to look.

CHAPTER THIRTY-TWO
Repossess Your Blessings

❖

I am sure you have heard the old saying that possession is 90% of ownership. In many ways this old axiom is right. No doubt being in possession of real property gives you an advantage in a title dispute. However, there are many ways for you to lose your right to property. When one owns property, there are conditions to be met, and a mortgage spells out those requirements. If the conditions are not met, then the title or right to that property begins to evaporate. We can very quickly find ourselves fighting for our house.

In the Old Testament, the Lord put a strong emphasis on land. Acquiring land. Securing land. Owning land. He even put a provision in place for getting your land back. Many of our bankruptcy laws in modern times come from the Old Testament. It appears that God wanted His children to have a place they could call their own. This was not unlike the principles that America was founded on. No doubt, America was established by men and women that read their Bible.

No doubt, America was established by men and women that read their Bible.

In the book of Leviticus, God instructs the people to have a grant of redemption for the land. *"The land shall not be sold for ever: for the land is mine; for ye are strangers and sojourners with me. And in all the land of your possession ye shall grant a redemption for the land."* (Leviticus 25:23-24). The dispute over land continues in the Middle East and much of that dispute comes from the belief that the land belongs to God and is only given to His people as a lease.

Redemption is the act of redeeming. Redeem means to free from a lien by a payment of an amount secured thereby. To free from captivity by payment of ransom. When something is redeemed it indicates prior ownership, not initial ownership. In the Old Testament the Lord said, *this land is mine. Forever! If times get tough or difficult and one has to sell it, I am establishing a law where one can get it back.*

Leviticus then continues with specific instructions for this grant of redemption. *"If thy brother be waxen poor, and hath sold away some of his possession, and if any of his kin come to redeem it, then shall he redeem that which his brother sold. And if the man have none to redeem it, and himself be able to redeem it; Then let him count the years of the sale thereof, and restore the overplus unto the man to whom he sold it; that he may return unto his possession."* (Leviticus 25:25-27)

If an individual came upon hard times and had to give up part of their land, they could have a relative, called a kinsmen redeemer, pay the debt and redeem the land. The kinsmen redeemer would hold the land for the person until they were able to recover it. The instructions in Leviticus went further into the redeeming business by instructing the seller of the land, or person who was in financial difficulty, to return to the buyer the money for the years it has been out of the seller's possession. When the seller accomplished this, the seller would be able to redeem the same land back into the seller's possession.

The term "quiet enjoyment" of your property was not around in the Bible times. **Now, when you get a "Fee Simple" title to your property, you have a right to "quiet enjoyment."** This means that you should be able to enjoy your property without having to worry about another claim to it or living in fear of it being taken away. The redemption laws of the Old Testament were based on the notion that no individual had exclusive rights to property because all property belongs to God originally.

If we can learn that God is the owner of our life and we are just sub-letting from Him, we will struggle less with our own will.

If redemption is the process of returning to the rightful owner a prior ownership, then the redemption of our salvation on Calvary was not an initial purchase of our salvation. When Jesus went to the cross and became the sacrifice for the sins of humanity, He was redeeming what rightfully belonged to Him in the first place.

The Bible says, *"The Earth is the Lord's and the fullness thereof."* (I Corinthians 10:26) A person is not their own, they are the property of their Creator. A life is on loan from God and can be recalled at any moment. Sin came in and kidnapped each of us, but the Lord paid the ransom note and redeemed us. If we can learn that God is the owner of our life and we are just subletting from Him, we will struggle less with our own will. The problem with our fleshly nature is that it wants to be in charge. Often times as a Youth Pastor, I would hear teenagers say, "When I turn 18, I am going to do my own thing." Somehow we think we are in charge of our own life, but actually it is just leased property of God.

The law from Leviticus continues by introducing the best of all redemption plans: the jubilee. "*But if he be not able to restore it to him, then that which is sold shall remain in the hand of him that hath bought it until the year of jubile: and in the jubile it shall go out, and he shall return unto his possession.*" (Leviticus 25:28) This year of jubilee was every 50 years. The year of jubilee was a year when one could get everything back whether it was affordable or not. In the jubilee year one could repossess his or her blessings. This was the time to rejoice for the return of all things. Not only did God have a redemption plan, but He also had a repossession plan.

Not only did God have a redemption plan, but He also had a repossession plan.

It was not by accident that the feast of Pentecost was celebrated fifty days after the Passover. The word Pentecost literally means fifty. This coincided with the year of jubilee. Something special happened in this period of time. It was not a coincidence that the Holy Spirit was poured out during the feast of Pentecost. (Acts 2:1) The Holy Spirit is a type of jubilee where we get our blessings back.

When we were born, we came into an environment that offered us innocence, hope, joy and love. These things are all on the face of a child. It is one reason why we are drawn to children. Over the course of time, we are hurt. We are hurt by people. We are injured by circumstances. We lose a little bit of that original innocence. One day at a time. One hurt at a time. Harsh words are said. Bitter feelings develop. Small things lodge in our spirit and become big. We lose our blessings one at a time; sometimes in bundles.

The Holy Spirit is our jubilee. The Holy Spirit restores to us everything that sin forced us to sell

The Holy Spirit restores to us everything that sin forced us to sell along the course of life.

along the course of life. Sin bankrupts us of all the blessings that God gave to us. God restores it to us through a redemption plan called jubilee. A redemption plan called the outpouring of the Holy Spirit. There is a way for us to repossess our blessings and the laws of property illustrate the truths of God's plan. Let's explore further.

CHAPTER THIRTY-THREE
Future Interests

❖

On July 6th, 1999 I arrived early for class. It was my second day of study with Chief Justice William Rehnquist at McGill University in Montreal. I was about twenty minutes early, but within five minutes the Chief walked in attired in his casual clothes with the same straw hat. When he took his hat off, he looked as if he had just awoken and his hair was quite unruly. I was amazed that he was early. The Chief sat down at his lecture table and waited for students to wander in to class. There was nothing pretentious about this man. He knew who he was, and he was comfortable in his aging skin. This Chief Justice of the U.S. Supreme Court knew that he was just a man. I wondered to myself if this is what the accumulation of years does for you as maturity puts everything into perspective.

At one point in the lecture, Chief Justice Rehnquist reminisced about the good fortune he had to become a member of the United States Supreme Court. He talked about how many talented people never have the chance to serve in such a place of honor. He did not believe it was because of their lack of expertise, but because of little insignificant factors. He commented that justices will tell you the main qualification to be a Supreme Court Justice is luck. "Be there when the bus goes by," the Chief commented. I think age must give you perspective that in the end your accomplishments were the result of good gifts and good fortune.

During one of our many discussions with the Chief, a fellow student was quite vocal in his criticism of a Supreme Court decision during World War II. The Chief allowed him to talk and when the student finished, the Chief said, "Your freedoms are not meant for just the present, they are meant to be preserved for future generations. Sometimes you give up a portion of your freedom today to ensure all of your freedoms for tomorrow." The class was quiet as those words marinated in our minds.

> "Your freedoms are not meant for just the present, they are meant to be preserved for future generations. Sometimes you give up a portion of your freedom today to ensure all of your freedoms for tomorrow."
> — **Chief Justice William Rehnquist**

Future interests is one of those areas of law that you either love or hate. Most students hate law school and are just trying to get through it. They want to graduate and get a good paying job. I was in a small category of students that really enjoyed the study of law and was not going to law school to get a job. I already knew what God had called me to do, and I was just having fun. I loved the study of law. I took to future interests like a fish to water. Each assignment was like a small riddle. "A" to "B" for as long as "B" shall live and then to "C." "B" has a present interest and "C" has a future interest.

A future interest has value, but because you don't have possession in the present, it can easily be discarded as worthless. In the modern age of microwave mentality, we think if we cannot enjoy it right now, then it cannot benefit us. The thought of delayed gratification is often lost on our youth when time is of the essence. Perhaps this is what caused Esau to sell his birthright for an instant bowl of soup. (Genesis 25:32)

A future interest is a right. It is an interest that will not vest or become a present interest until either the testator dies or the owner of the present interest passes it on. The testator is the original grantor who has granted the property rights. The testator is usually the trigger that can make the property move and pass to the intended parties.

Hebrews 9 gives us some insight into the identity of Jesus. "*And for this cause he is the mediator of the new testament, that by means of death, for the redemption of the transgressions that were under the first testament, they which are called might receive the promise of eternal inheritance. **For where a testament is, there must also of necessity be the death of the testator.** For a testament is of force after men are dead: otherwise it is of no strength at all while the testator liveth.*" (Hebrews 9:15-17)

For Calvary to be a legal transfer of the redemption rights of our transgressions, the one who dies had to be of the same essence of the original testator. The testator had to die for the redemption right to move. If we ever had any doubts of who Jesus is, that should clear it up. There had to be a death and it had to be the testator. The testator is the one who has the authority.

A contingent remainder interest is an interest that is present, but it has contingencies. ("A" to "B" as long as "B" continues to stay in school, pays his bills, and eats his vegetables. "B" has a contingent remainder interest.) There are conditions that have to be met for the interest to remain. To make things more interesting, a contingent remainder interest can be called a Fee Simple Determinable with a Possibility of Reverter or a Fee Simple Subject to Condition Subsequent based on the way it is structured.

A Fee Simple Determinable automatically terminates when the condition is not met and goes back to the grantor. A Fee Simple Subject to Condition Subsequent continues until the grantor exercises his or her power and takes it back. A Fee Simple Determinable grantor can be passive, and the rights will return, but a Fee Simple Subject to Condition Subsequent grantor must be proactive for the rights to return.

II Chronicles 7:14 says, " *If my people, which are called by my name, shall humble themselves, and pray, and seek my face, and turn from their wicked ways; then will I hear from heaven, and will forgive their sin, and will heal their land.*" It would appear that this promise has a contingent remainder interest. It has stipulations. There is something that is required of us.

> The grantor of this gift called salvation has given us a present interest and a future interest.

I Timothy 4:16 says, "*Take heed unto thyself, and unto the doctrine; continue in them: for in doing this thou shalt both save thyself, and them that hear thee.*" The words "continue in them" would indicate that this contingency has to continue for the promise to be valid. The grantor of this gift called salvation has given us a present interest and a future interest. While one could argue that God is passive in the reverting back of a present interest, one cannot deny that both interests require that we heed the Biblical instructions.

Let's flip the table of application, and use God's Word to instruct us as to how passive or proactive we must be to take back what belongs to us. A Fee Simple Subject to Condition Subsequent requires that the grantor exercise his power and take it back. This is what happened when the keys to death and hell were taken back from Satan by God at Calvary. (Revelation 1:18) The Bible says that Jesus descended first into the lower parts of the earth before He ascended and went to heaven. (Ephesians 4:9) That is the grantor exercising his power and taking it back.

The Old Testament is replete with instructions from God to the Children of Israel to "take the land." Be proactive and take what was rightfully given. If the enemy has taken some of our territory, or if he has invaded our homes and stolen our children or our finances, we have a legal and a biblical right to exercise our authority and take back what rightfully belongs to us. God promised, in Joel 2:25, that He would *"restore to you the years that the locust hath eaten, the cankerworm, and the caterpillar, and the palmerworm."*

Why wait for the rights to revert back? Why not exercise your authority now by declaring the name of Jesus. That is what the apostles were doing in the book of Acts. They were going into the synagogues and taking back what belonged to them in the first place. Your health, your joy, your peace. It was yours in the beginning. Take it back.

CHAPTER THIRTY-FOUR
Adverse Possession

❖

I continued to study under the tutelage of the Chief Justice of the United States Supreme Court, William Rehnquist. The Chief, as we began to call him affectionately, had become familiar with the names of a few of the students that spoke in class frequently. He welcomed this participation and took great pains to remember our names. He called me Mr. Myers and always asked me to brief a case to get the ball rolling in class each day.

On Thursday the 15th of July 1999, the Chief was wrapping up his lectures and opened up the floor for us to ask him anything that we wanted concerning the Supreme Court. He cautioned that he could not comment on any case or issue that would possibly be before the Court, but everything else was fair game. I got the first question in; I asked him about the impeachment trial that he had presided over in the recent months for President Clinton. He hesitated to answer and everyone laughed. Slowly he said, "It was a political process that some of my close friends from other countries have told me would not have been a big deal in their country, but I believe that it worked according to the way the Constitution intended." He was careful not to show any bias or disappointment.

Other students asked about his law school experience, his plans for retirement and procedural practices of the Supreme Court. Some even asked about his advice for them and their legal careers. The Chief was very forthright and seemed to be enjoying the questions. He was not apologetic about refusing to answer questions that he preferred not to address. It was a casual atmosphere of humor and insight. As time was coming to a close, I thought about a couple of questions that I could ask such as, "What do you like most about being a Chief Justice and what do you like least?" I decided against this question and went for the jugular.

The remaining minutes of our time with the Chief Justice were ticking away. I raised my hand and the Chief acknowledged me by name. I asked, "In your book you mentioned that Franklin D. Roosevelt had regular poker games in the basement of the White House with friends and colleagues, and there are rumors that similar poker games continue today with justices and politicians involved. If that is true, how would you avoid a conflict of interest?"

He was visibly shaken by the question, but it was a legitimate question. It was based on information I had from Justice Scalia about the Chief and important political figures that have ongoing poker games in Washington. This questionable practice of playing a game with people who you may have to decide on the constitutionality of their congressional bill had flown under the radar for many years.

The Chief Justice's eyes darted back and forth as he searched for his hat. He said in a very uneven voice, "I think that is one of those questions that I will not answer." There was an invisible, yet very prevalent heavy cloud that filled the room. He took one little quick question and answered it in two sentences as he adjusted his hat on his head. He then wished us well and walked to the door. I stood to applaud him and a couple of others joined, but most of the students didn't bother.

Afterwards, students came up to me and said, "Great question!" They talked about how the Chief made it look more ominous by not answering the question. I agreed with the assessment, but I felt badly. I did ask a direct question to see what his response would be, but I had not intended to make him that uncomfortable. Some of the students were joking about how the Internal Revenue Service would be auditing me now. I had mixed feelings. On one hand, I felt that since he asks tough questions all the time to the best attorneys in the country, he should be able to handle tough questions. On the other hand, I felt like I put him in a bad light in front of a group of students that he had just finished teaching, and that was not necessary. I thought he would be able to handle the question, after all, he is the Chief Justice. No doubt I worried about it more than he did, but somehow I felt like I had taken advantage of an elderly man that I genuinely admired. It seems that an easy answer for the Chief in response to my question would have been, "What conflict of interest?"

A fellow student came to me afterward and said the New Yorker magazine had run an article that said sometimes Kenneth Starr, the

Independent Counsel that investigated President Clinton, would join the poker game with the Chief. This of course, if true, could pose serious conflict of interest questions. Whatever it was, I touched a nerve and any hopes that I had of being a law clerk for the Chief Justice of the United States Supreme Court quickly dissipated.

I suppose there are few conflict of interest issues that are more on point as to the conflict than the legal theory of adverse possession. When someone is living on land that you own without your permission, there is certainly a conflict of interest. **Barron's Law Dictionary, Third Edition, defines adverse possession as "a method of acquiring complete title to land as against all others, including the record owner, through certain acts over an uninterrupted period of time as prescribed by statute."** It is usually prescribed that such possession must be actual, visible, open, notorious, hostile, under claim of right, definite, continuous and exclusive.

This legal right to acquire property is sometimes loosely referred to as squatter's rights. The law was put in place to encourage people who have property to take care of it. The law wants an individual to look after their land and not to be an absentee owner. If someone owns something then there are responsibilities that go with the title. If the owner abandons it and someone else comes in and meets the requirements, the law says we will transfer title to them. In theory, this is what the law is saying, but in practice taking title through adverse possession is not easily accomplished.

The spiritual application of this principle is more easily accomplished. There is no doubt that God has given us title to some spiritual ground that He expects us to occupy. There is also no doubt that our enemy is hostile and will fight us for the right to that property. The Lord gives us children as a gift, and we are instructed to raise them in the fear of God, but if we don't, the enemy will. The Lord gives us freedoms and dominion over the prince and power of the air (Ephesians 2:2), but if we don't exercise those rights, we can easily lose them.

There is no doubt that God has given us title to some spiritual ground that He expects us to occupy.

The laws of adverse possession require that you openly resist the adverse possessor. You have to remove them from your property. In *Van Valkenburgh v. Lutz*, 304 N.Y. 95, 106 N.E. 2nd 28 (1952), the court held that an adverse possessor who walked across the property of another on a continuous basis, built a shed on it and kept a garden on it without opposition from the title owner, had legal right to title of the property after the statutory period of time was completed.

If we allow the enemy to walk all over our promises, then he is going to try and take possession.

If we allow the enemy to walk all over our promises, then he is going to try and take possession. If we allow the enemy to build a place of residence, even a small place, on our property, then he will get a foothold in our family. If we are going to sit down with the enemy and play card games, then we are going to lose our ability to exclude him from our lives and the lives of our family members.

If your neighbor puts up a fence on your property, you better resist. If you don't, that fence can become the new boundary regardless of what the survey says. Every time a movie is played or a show is watched in our home that is inappropriate, the enemy has moved a little more into our home. Every time a song is listened to that is hostile to the principles of God's Word, the boundaries are moved a little closer. Before we know it, the new boundary is the established line and we are cohabitating with the enemy. That is why the Bible says, *"Remove not the ancient landmark."* (Proverbs 22:28)

The key to driving out adverse possessors is found in one simple word; resist. *"Resist the devil and he will flee from you."* (James 4:7) Resist the onslaught of evil. Resist the encroachment of ungodly principles. Resist the erosion of family values. If you resist the adversary, you will retain the authority.

CHAPTER THIRTY-FIVE
Life Estate

❖

My wife and I were discussing the need for a larger vehicle with the soon arrival of our daughter. Our twin five-year-old sons were in the back seat, and they were listening to our conversation. My wife was making the case that we needed a vehicle with two rows of seats in the back to accommodate the growing family with luggage and strollers and additional paraphernalia. Then she added, "The boys are getting bigger every day and they are going to need a lot of room."

I thought I would have some fun so I said, "What if we quit feeding them? If we quit feeding them, they won't get any bigger." My wife joined in and said, "Yeah, I guess we could do that. Let's quit feeding them and we won't need a new car." It was quiet in the back seat only for a few moments, when one of our sons cleared his voice and said, "Uh, Dad, I am pretty sure I am going to need to eat every day." After laughing, I thought how true it is of our spiritual needs. I am pretty sure we need the Lord every day of our life.

A life estate is an estate that is granted to a person for the span of their life or the span of someone else's life. "A" will go to "B" as long as "B" shall live and then it goes to "C." "B" has a life estate. "A" will go to "B" as long as "C" shall live, and then it will go to "D." "B" still has a life estate, only now it is measured by the life of "C." A life estate will not pass on to heirs after the person whose life is being measured passes. It is not a future right, it is a present right. A Fee Simple estate that an individual usually receives when they buy a piece of real estate has a bundle of rights that includes both present and future interests. **The life estate interest is void of the future interest because it only runs during the life of the measured individual.**

There were times in scripture when God gave a promise specifically for the life of the individual that He desired to bless. An example of this is found in Joshua 1:5, *"There shall not any man be able to stand before thee all the days of thy life: as I was with Moses, so I will be with thee: I will not fail thee, nor forsake thee."* This promise was specific to Moses for his life and this promise was specific to Joshua for his life. They were *life* promises. Just as a man or woman could receive a life sentence for a crime that does not pass to the heirs, so does God give a life promise to individuals that runs only for their life span.

It is important to understand that God has a present interest in the quality of our life. He has a map and a plan for our specific life. There are principles of God's Word that are universal, but there is also a plan of God that is custom made for our life. It has been said that there are four things we need to be happy in life:

1. Something to do
2. Someone to love
3. Something to hope for
4. Someone to believe in

If life could be boiled down to these four essentials, then Jesus Christ can meet each of these needs in your life.

If we want God to direct our every step, then we have to take measures to incorporate Him into the affairs of our life.

II Corinthians 4:16 says, *"For which cause we faint not; but though our outward man perish, yet the inward man is renewed day by day."* How is the inward man renewed day by day? Is it with materialism? Is it with personal friendships or achievements? Is it vitamins? Certainly all of those things can give us a sense of well being if even for a short period of time. However, there is a day-to-day process of incorporating God into our lives that renews us.

This day-by-day process of keeping God in our life is what we do to keep the *life* promises of God active in our life. If we want God to direct our every step, then we have to take measures to incorporate Him into the affairs of our life. God is a gentleman. He does not barge in. He waits. He watches. He listens. He knocks. He is not bound and determined to override our own free will, but He does desire to bless us every day of our life in a special way.

I think the Lord knew we would need this daily dose of God in our life, because early on he gave this precedent to the children of

Israel. Consider these Old Testament scriptures. Exodus 13:21 says, *"And the LORD went before them by day in a pillar of a cloud, to lead them the way; and by night in a pillar of fire, to give them light; to go by day and night."* Exodus 29:38 says, *"Now this is that which thou shalt offer upon the altar; two lambs of the first year day by day continually."* Ezra 3:4 says *"They kept also the feast of tabernacles, as it is written, and offered the daily burnt offerings by number, according to the custom, as the duty of every day required."* God gives us some basic life instructions from the Word of God so that our time on earth will be savored and satisfying on a daily basis.

1. Daily Prayer

Part of having this life estate where God blesses your life on a daily basis is to make sure you find time each day to talk to the Lord. This daily time of prayer will keep the communication lines open so that God can continue to talk to you and dwell with you.

2. Daily Praise

David said in Psalms 145:2, *"Every day will I bless thee; and I will praise thy name forever and ever."* David was known for praising daily. We should find something to praise God for every day. This daily praise will keep us in a frame of mind that will bring higher quality to our life. We will begin to see what God has for us in this estate called life.

3. Daily Petition

In the New Testament, when the disciples asked Jesus to teach them to pray, He gave them a model prayer. Part of this model prayer is found in Luke 11:3, *"Give us day by day our daily bread."* We often think that we are bugging God when we bring our petitions to Him. It is actually just the opposite. God views our petitions as an act of faith. When we bring our needs to God on a daily basis, we are confessing our faith every day.

4. Daily Perspective

I'm sure I need God every day. Even though I have food to eat; I need God. Even though I have a place to sleep; I need God. Even though I have money in my pocket; I need God. Even though I am not sick; I need God. Even though I have friends and I have a job; I need God. I'm sure every day, and with every breath; I need God. Perspective is recognizing our utter dependence on the grantor of our life. This life that is on loan from God is not my own.

5. Daily Purpose

Psalms 7:11 says, "*God judgeth the righteous, and God is angry with the wicked every day.*" Every day, God is angry with the wicked. Be aware that you are under attack every day. If God fights this battle every day, so will you. As long as you are fighting it, you are winning. If you are not fighting it, you are losing it. You have to have a purpose to your life. God has a specific plan for your life, but you must seize it with these daily disciplines.

On a frigid January morning in a small Wisconsin town that hugged the southern shore of Lake Superior, the annual dog sled derby was about to begin. A one mile course had been staked out by sticking little fir trees on the ice. The whole course was easily visible because of the steep slope on the shore.

It was an organized race for the youth in the community and the contenders ranged from large boys with several dogs and big sleds to one little fellow who didn't seem over five years old with a little sled and one dog. They took off at the signal and the little fellow with one dog was quickly outdistanced; he was hardly in the race. All went well with the rest until about halfway around the tract, the team that was in second started to past the team that was leading. They came too close and the dogs got into a fight. As each team came up to pass, their dogs joined the fight. Soon it was just one big seething mass of kids, sleds, and dogs.

When it appeared that the race would have to be cancelled, the little boy with one dog that everyone had forgotten about managed to steer his dog around the confusion and just kept going. He ended up winning the race because he was the only one that finished the race.

Life will offer a lot of struggles, a lot of challenges, and a lot of unexpected circumstances. When it does, remember the little boy with one dog in a little town on the shores of Lake Superior. Regardless how difficult the challenge is or how impossible the task may seem, if one is reasonably sure of their course, just keep on going. I am sure God will help each of us every day for the duration of our life.

CHAPTER THIRTY-SIX
Rule Against Perpetuities

❖

If you ask any attorney what they dread more than anything else in law school, the common answer is, "The Rule against Perpetuities." This rule is known for being confusing, irrelevant, archaic, and basically something that needs to be forgotten. Now doesn't that make you want to learn more about it?

The Rule against Perpetuities says that, "No contingent interest is good unless it must vest, if at all, not later than twenty one years after some life in being at the creation of the interest." (Black's Law Dictionary, Third Edition) If the future interest is going to be measured by someone's life, then it has to be within twenty-one years of a person who is alive at the time of the creation of the interest. The rule basically means future interests that give endless, perpetual ownership rights have limits.

This law wants to limit the endless future interests that can drag out forever. This was the rule they came up with to be able to keep a measuring stick on the length of time the interest is intended to run. That is man's law, but it did not originate with man.

The law of redemption had boundaries. Leviticus 25:29-31 says, *"And if a man sell a dwelling house in a walled city, then he may redeem it within a whole year after it is sold; within a full year may he redeem it. And if it be not redeemed within the space of a full year, then the house that is in the walled city shall be established for ever to him that bought it throughout his generations: it shall not go out in the jubilee. But the houses of the villages which have no wall round about them shall be counted as the fields of the country: they may be redeemed, and they shall go out in the jubilee."*

If you sold something that was protected by the walls, you could redeem it within a year, but if you did not, you lost it forever. This is the same principle as *"to whom much is given, much is required."* (Luke 12:48).

If you have been raised in a Christian home, you are a blessed individual. If you know what it is like to have the walls of prayer and the walls of morality, then you should count your blessings. Sometimes it is easy to take those things for granted because you don't know the value of the walls. Sometimes you begin to resent the walls. As a teenager, I remember hearing my mother pray for me as I left to drive to high school. I would silently wish that her prayers were directed toward someone else in the church. Our house was inside of the walls.

If in your haste to explore the world outside of the walls, you sell that inheritance, then get it back quick. You do not have an endless amount of time to redeem your godly heritage. The world outside of the walls will take a toll on you if you let it go beyond the space of repentance. Beyond a time when your heart can still be reconciled, you run the risk of losing it forever.

You can't measure God with time or space.

God has some laws that say, "This is the way it is, and this is the way it will always be. Forever!" Our God *"is able to do exceeding abundantly above all that we ask or think..."* (Ephesians 3:20). You can't measure God with time or space.

God gave the children of Israel a promise that was to run continually. *"And the LORD said to Abram, after Lot had separated from him: Lift your eyes now and look from the place where thou art northward, southward, eastward, and westward; for all the land which you see I give to you and your descendants forever."* (Gen 13:14-15) This interest that God was giving to the children of Israel was not a limited estate. It was not a promise that was only good during the life of Moses. The promise was a perpetual promise.

Many of the promises that God gives to us are not limited to just our own life, but also go to the lives of our children. The Psalmist David said, *"I have been young, and now am old; yet have I not seen the righteous forsaken, nor his seed begging bread."* (Psalms 37:25) Peter said, *"For the promise is unto you and to your children and to those that are afar off, even as many as the Lord our God shall call."* (Acts 2:39) These promises are not simply a promise for life, but they travel down to our heirs much like a fee simple estate would.

The mercy and love of God is limitless, but the condition of the heart of man is not.

God does not have a limited supply of mercy. His mercy endureth forever. God does not have a limited supply of forgiveness. The Lord is the same yesterday, today, and forever. This may seem like a contradiction to the limited time that people had to redeem their houses inside of the walls. This may seem like a contradiction to the fact that Esau was not able to find repentance and redeem his inheritance (Hebrews 12:17), but it is not. The mercy and love of God is limitless, but the condition of the heart of man is not.

That's redemption; a second chance at something that was ours in the first place.

When the Children of Israel were given the promise land, Palestine, the Lord wanted to give them an endless inheritance. Something that would stay in the family forever, but because He knows that His people are human and we don't always realize the value of something, He made a way where one could mess up, make a bad decision and still get back what was meant for them in the first place. That's redemption; a second chance at something that was ours in the first place.

Though mercy and forgiveness is what drives us to be redeemed, there are seasons in our life when we are open to this salvation and seasons when we are out of reach. Time is of the essence and God knows us better than we know ourselves. God knew that we would have to strike when the iron was hot or miss our opportunity to come back home. Not because of His limited love, but rather because of our limited time.

THE WILL

An Inheritance that Probate Court Cannot Control

❖

We have all heard the great stories about a rich uncle that left a million dollars to an unsuspecting nephew. Perhaps, we have even dreamed of some long lost uncle leaving us his estate in the hills of Hawaii, but most of us never see that kind of favorable Will. In fact, most of us never even think about making our own Will. We know that one day we will die, but we hate to get too prepared for it because that may speed up the process.

I am never real excited when they call from the cemetery and want to sell me a cemetery plot. I know I may need one in the future, but since my hope is in the scripture, I think more about leasing a cemetery plot than buying one. In any event, preparing for death is not an easy process to wrap your mind around.

Among all of the wonderful benefits of living by the Word of God, one that is often overlooked is the blessing of having a Will or plan for the future that goes beyond death. The Scripture goes beyond just giving you direction for this life; it gives you assurance for the life to come. It prepares a path that has a road map for eternity. The scriptures give us a Will that is more favorable than a rich uncle leaving us a million dollars; it gives us a written conveyance of treasures and security.

Paul recorded in Acts 20:32, *"The Word of His grace is able to build you up and give you an inheritance."* I am glad to know that not only do I need a Will for the natural things of this life; I also need a spiritual Will that will prepare my estate for eternity. I need to know that God has within His Word the guidance for this transition. The good news is we will see how the laws of our land concerning natural Wills parallel the laws of God concerning spiritual Wills.

The exciting event of reading the Will is lost on those that do not see the Word of God as a reading of a favorable Will, but it is exactly that. Let's read the Will (God's Word) and see what is in store for us.

CHAPTER THIRTY-SEVEN
What's In the Will?

❖

In 1904, the average life expectancy in the United States was forty-seven. Only 14 percent of the homes in the United States had a bathtub. Only 8 percent of the homes had a telephone. A three-minute call from Denver to New York City cost eleven dollars. There were only 8,000 cars in the United States and only 144 miles of paved roads. Sugar cost four cents a pound. Eggs were fourteen cents a dozen. Coffee cost fifteen cents a pound. The population of Las Vegas, Nevada was 30. Crossword puzzles and iced tea were not yet invented, and one in ten U.S. adults could not read or write.

What value was in the last 100 plus years? What is so valuable that our forefathers gave us? It is not the money or the education, but it is the morals. It is the Book. It is the Truth. It is the outpouring of the Holy Ghost. That's what is in the Will, and that is priceless.

In most states if you die intestate, or without a Will, the state will attempt to find an equitable way to distribute assets. The first priority is to look for a surviving spouse. If a surviving spouse is not found, the next priority is lineal descendents or children, natural or adopted. The next priority is lineal ascendants, such as surviving parents and then collateral heirs which are siblings.

If a Will is established, then you can leave your estate to whomever you choose. God is so good He covers us either way. God established His Word as the Will. The Bible is a legal document comprised of two testaments, but the Word also gives us the legal guidance of a statutory document. I am sure you have heard the term, Last Will and Testament. The Bible is a Will and a Testament of where and how God will bestow His blessings. In case there is any

God established His Word as the Will.

doubt about this document, God also covers the intestate side of legal distribution by incorporating us into His family.

In John 1:12 we read, *"But as many as received him, to them gave he power to become the sons of God, even to them that believe on his name."* There was a power or an authority that was given to make us as humans the sons of God. The first thing that we have to identify in a Will is the parties. We have to give proof of identity to even be in the reading. If one is a named participant, but a Will was not written, the relationship to the deceased will have to be proven.

The Spirit of God gave us legal power to become the sons of God.

As a doctor of the Law, Paul understood this and made several legal references to our relationship with God. Paul knew that God's plan called for a legal recipient of the treasures of Heaven. There was a testator and a testament, but the plan of God needed some heirs. In Romans 8:14 Paul said *"For as many as are led by the Spirit of God, they are the sons of God."* The Spirit of God gave us legal power to become the sons of God.

In Romans 8:15-17, Paul makes the case even stronger by clearly communicating the nature of our relationship with the Father for legal purposes. *"For ye have not received the spirit of bondage again to fear; but ye have received the Spirit of adoption, whereby we cry, Abba, Father. The Spirit itself beareth witness with our spirit, that we are the children of God: And if children, then heirs; heirs of God, and joint-heirs with Christ; if so be that we suffer with him, that we may be also glorified together."*

This is the legal authority that God establishes so that we can become heirs of Him. It is also why the disciples attached themselves to the name of Jesus in the ministry of the early church recorded in Acts. They prayed for the sick in Jesus' name, they cast out devils in Jesus' name, and they baptized in Jesus' name. This name gives us the authority of relationship. Not only is this important for spiritual warfare, it is vital to the spiritual Will.

Paul spoke on this same theme in Acts 20 when he said what the Will would do for us. Acts 20:32 says the Word of His grace will build you up and give you an inheritance. A person can work all of his life and never get ahead. Then suddenly receive word that a Will has been left from a distant relative entitling his family to thousands of dollars. That kind of news will change one's life. The Will that God has for us is not just a monetary amount or a promise of future possessions; it is the ability to have each day of our life count. It is daily strength. It is daily hope. It is daily purpose.

We can work hard all our life and just be in a big mess trying to get ahead outside of the Word. However, when we turn to the Will, the Book, the Testament, and we find out what is in the Will, we really start living then. Life starts to turn around. Life starts to make sense. You know it is of value because thieves are going to try and steal it. Paul said as soon as I depart, grievous wolves are going to come in and try to steal the treasure. (Acts 20:29)

In Acts 2, when Peter was explaining to the crowd that had gathered for the demonstration of the covenant, what all this noise was about, he said *"these men are not drunk as ye suppose, seeing it is but the third hour of the day. But this is that that was spoken by the prophet Joel....."* (Acts 2:15-16). It's in the Will. It's in your Law. It was spoken of by your prophets.

The Holy Spirit of God not only provides legal transfer of the blessings of God, it also provides the value of the Will by empowering you and I to enjoy the benefits of it. Everything about God. Every good gift. Every promise. It's all in the Will.

If an heir cannot be found, the possessions of the estate will escheat back to the State. Millions of dollars are lost every year because of unclaimed assets. The possessions revert back to the State. Don't be absent for the reading of the Will. We don't want to change our identity and lose our spiritual heritage. There are too many things in the Will that are specially designated just for us.

CHAPTER THIRTY-EIGHT
Pretermitted Children

❖

Pretermitted children are children born after the Will was executed, or children adopted after the Will of the adoptive parent or parents was executed. In Florida, as in most states, there are special laws to protect these children that might have been forgotten. Every state, except Louisiana, does not require that individuals leave anything to their children, not even the proverbial one dollar. People may disinherit their children entirely. The exception is pretermitted children.

If the testator omits to provide in his or her Will for any of his or her children, biological or adopted, after the Will is executed, the children have legal rights to the estate. These rights are an entitlement to a share equal in value to what they would have received if the testator had died intestate…without a Will. [F.P.C. 732.302] There are exceptions to this rule such as if the child is intentionally and specifically omitted. The state will not force individuals to gift to anyone, only to fill in the gaps of where they anticipate that a child may have been forgotten.

Suffice it to say that pretermitted children are born after the Will has been arranged and they are protected under most state statutes so they are included in the Will. This is very similar to what Paul was speaking about in Romans when he talked about the Gentiles coming into the covenant with God after it had been executed with the Jews. The Jews had a difficult time even accepting the fact that the Gentiles could be saved. Paul, understanding this phenomenon, taught on the subject as he attempted to bridge the gap between the Jews and the Gentiles.

"Even us, whom he hath called, not of the Jews only, but also of the Gentiles? As he saith also in Osee (Hosea), I will call them my people, which were not my people; and her beloved, which was not beloved. And it shall come to pass,

that in the place where it was said unto them, Ye are not my people; there shall they be called the children of the living God." (Romans 9:24-26) Paul quoting the Old Testament prophet Hosea stated that there would be a people that would come afterward, and they would be a part of the original covenant.

This was further illustrated as Paul expounded on the subject. *"And if some of the branches be broken off, and thou, being a wild olive tree, were grafted in among them, and with them partakest of the root and fatness of the olive tree..."* (Romans 11:17). He then cautioned the Gentiles that even though there has been provision made for them under the original Will, they should not feel exclusive or high-minded about their status. *"For if thou wert cut out of the olive tree which is wild by nature, and were grafted contrary to nature into a good olive tree: how much more shall these, which be the natural branches, be grafted into their own olive tree?"* (Romans 11:24).

Paul understood the pretermitted status of God's children. He even referred to himself as *"one born out of due time."* (1 Corinthians 15:8) Paul understood that sometimes you feel like you do not belong to the family of God because of what you did in your past. He goes on to explain in the following verse that he is not worthy because he persecuted the church. Paul dealt with a lot of condemnation because of his past. No doubt, Paul felt like he did not deserve all of the blessings that God had bestowed on him.

People may feel that they are not fit to be a part of God's inheritance. Numerous times I have heard people say that they could never be saved because of what they have done in their youth or because of some terrible sin in their past. But God has a plan where the wild olive branch is grafted into the church. He has a plan where the children that are born out of due time are still protected under the Law. People may not feel like they belong, but God has made legal provision where not only do these individuals belong, but they are provided additional protection against exclusion.

The statutes in Florida, as in most states, make specific reference to the fact that adopted children are to be treated the same as natural children of the adoptive parents. [F.P.C. 732.108] The adopted child can inherit from and through his or her adoptive parents and the adoptive parents and their kin can inherit from and through the adoptive child. The relationship is the same between parent and child in terms of

There is not any temptation that has authority over us.

the law and the rules on intestacy. Paul said, *"We have received the spirit of adoption, whereby we cry Abba Father,"* or daddy. (Romans 8:15).

The relationship that we have with our heavenly Father is not only a legal relationship for purposes of the law honoring our right to inherit, but we also can have a loving relationship that is not void of intimacy. Paul must have learned this in his own life. He found that God did not hold his past against him. If God did not hold Paul's past against him, he will not hold our past against us.

For purposes of inheritance, an adopted child *"is not a lineal descendant of his natural parents nor is he one of the kindred of any member of his natural parents' family."* [F.P.C. 732.108] Thus, when a child is adopted by a new family, the adopted child and his kin have no inheritance rights from or through his natural parents, and the natural parents and their kin have no inheritance rights from or through the natural child who has been adopted. In a spiritual sense, once we come to the Lord and you take on the identity of His name, our legal connection with the past life is cut off.

You and I do not owe sin anything. You and I do not owe our carnal nature anything. We may be born in sin, but we don't have to die in sin. There is not anything in the "carnal man" that can take authority over the "spiritual man." There is not any temptation that has authority over us. We don't inherit the weaknesses of our natural father; we inherit the strengths of our spiritual Father. The enemy cannot benefit from us. We have been adopted into the royal line of God's provision.

We have been adopted into the royal line of God's provision.

In Florida, *"heirs of the decedent conceived before his death but born thereafter inherit intestate property as if they had been born during the decedent's lifetime."* [F.P.C. 732.106] This classification is called posthumous children. Jesus said *"You must be born again."* (John 3:3). Our birth into Christ has taken place since the crucifixion. It takes place after our natural birth, but it does not change our status with God. Our natural birth was the design and creation of God, but our spiritual birth, subsequent to Calvary, puts us in the middle of God's mighty hand of inheritance.

CHAPTER THIRTY-NINE
Holographic Will

❖

A story is told of a grandchild that was missing her grandparents. The little girl attempted to explain to her friends what had happened to her grandparents since they retired and moved to Florida. "We always spend our vacation with Grandma and Grandpa. They used to live here in a big, brick house, but Grandpa got tired and they moved to Florida and now they live in a place with a lot of other tired people. They ride around on big tricycles and go to a building called a 'wrecked center.' They must have fixed the building because it is all right now.

At their gate, is a playhouse with a little, old man sitting in it. He watches all day so nobody can escape. Some of the people can't get past the man in the playhouse to go out, so the ones who get out bring food back to the wrecked center and call it pot luck. My Grandma says Grandpa worked all his life to earn being tired and says I should work hard so I can be tired one day, too. When I earn being tired, I want to be the man in the playhouse. Then I will let people out so they can visit their grandchildren."

Now we know how some children look at the retirement centers. I thought about how things sometimes look so different on the surface than how they are in reality. One may think that a Will must be typed, double-spaced, and placed in plastic protectors to be valid, but actually anyone can just write out a Will on the back of a envelope, and in many cases, if it is signed, it is valid.

A Holographic Will is a Will entirely in the testator's handwriting and signed by the testator, but not witnessed by attesting witnesses. The Uniform Probate Code and many states give effect

The Bible is more reliable than the documents in our legal system that we are accepting of as valid.

to Holographic Wills. This is based on a public policy issue to encourage people to write out a Will. Some states, like Florida, acknowledge handwritten Wills, but require a signature of the testator and two witnesses. This type of Will would not by definition be a Holographic Will because it has witnesses.

The Bible says that "*No prophecy of scripture is of private interpretation but holy men of God spoke as they were moved on by the Holy Ghost*" (II Peter 1:20-21). It may appear at first glance that the Bible could be interpreted as a Holographic Will because it is all written by the Spirit of God. One could even argue that it is hand signed with the finger print of His blood, but the Bible has so many witnesses it easily moves into the category of a document evidenced with undeniable proof.

A Will can be contested for many things including, but not limited to, fraud, mistake, testamentary capacity, and undue influence. Each of these issues make a Holographic Will more susceptible to challenges. The Bible seems to go out of its way to offer proof of its assertions. The Bible is more reliable than the documents in our legal system that we are accepting of as valid.

Everything about God is that of substantiating Himself and His Word. This is where the legal nature of God is on display with such clarity. It is not easy to find independent proof when you are God. A witness cannot compare to the author. The scriptures say in Hebrews 6:13 that when God made a covenant with Abraham, "*he could sware by no greater so he sware by himself.*" The amazing aspect of this verse is that God would look for a witness. That depicts the nature of God.

God is into proof. He offers evidence of His existence and He offers proof of His power. He has witnesses of His Word. We have to work hard to not believe in God. Six times in the Old and New Testament the phrase "*two or three witnesses*" is found. Each time the context is found to confirm or give credibility. Mathew 18:16 says that "*In the mouth of two or three witnesses, let every word be established.*" The multitude of witnesses that God gives goes overboard to establish each word and every work.

The multitude of witnesses that God gives goes overboard to establish each word and every work.

Paul continued on this theme as he witnessed to Governor Festus and King Agrippa in Acts 26:26. Paul stated to these political leaders that "*this thing was not done in a corner.*" The gospel was not being spread in an underground covert fashion. The works of God are apparent to everyone. The outpouring of the Holy Ghost in Acts 2 spilled out into the street with thousands of visitors. The miracles of Jesus were witnessed by thousands. Many other faiths are based on the account of one man who saw or felt something that cannot be independently verified. God does not require such blind faith. God gives witnesses to the Will.

We are witnesses to the greatest message that has ever reached the ears of humanity. Sometimes we witness the miraculous and don't identify the miracle in the mundane. We have a lot of messages that invade our minds on a daily basis. Some of these messages are wrapped with appeal that is unforgettable. Some are not what they appear to be. God deals with sustenance over style. It may appear to just be a book, but it has the words of life. It may appear to just be another church service, but it could change our life. It may appear to just be a one-sided conversation, but it may give us strength for the storm.

Sometimes we witness the miraculous and don't identify the miracle in the mundane.

It may appear to be a strange conglomerate of elderly folks doing unexplained activities, similar to the child that could not understand what her grandparents were doing in a retirement center in Florida. It may appear to only be a handwritten note on the back of an envelope, but if it is signed, it could be a Holographic Will recognized by the state. It may appear to be just the zealous nature of uneducated fisherman, but the council that gathered in Acts 4 to judge and punish these men had to declare that, *"Indeed a notable miracle hath been done here and we can not deny it."*

The witnesses that God gives of the miraculous should give us a confidence that God does not prove himself with smoke and mirrors, He proves himself over and over with witnesses whose changed lives speak for themselves throughout history.

CHAPTER FORTY
The Codicil

❖

I have never been able to make any money in the stock market, but I am told that if you can anticipate mergers, you can make some quick money if you buy ahead of the merger, and then cash out after the merger. At the risk of insider trading laws being violated, I would like to share with you some rumors of mergers that may be beneficial.

Hale Business Systems, Mary Kay Cosmetics, Fuller Brush, and W. R. Grace Company will merge and become: Hale, Mary, Fuller, Grace. Polygram Records, Warner Brothers. and Zesta Crackers may join forces and become: Poly, Warner Cracker. FedEx is expected to join its major competitor, UPS, and become: FedUP. This is also how our congregation feels when I unleash another lame joke. The merger of companies or testaments must be completed correctly to be sustainable.

A codicil is a later testamentary instrument that amends, alters, or modifies a previously executed Will. A codicil must be executed with the same testamentary formalities as a Will. If the testator has decided to add heirs to benefit from the final disposition of assets, they do not have to create an entirely new Will; they can just amend it through a codicil. This is a useful tool because Wills are very fluid and often change.

There is no doubt that the New Testament has a different tone than the Old Testament. This dichotomy often raises questions as to how the same God could have been the author of both testaments. The Old Testament appears to be focused on the law and the New Testament seems to be focused on forgiveness and mercy. This even drew questions from the Pharisees who were well-educated in the law, but were not able to understand and accept the teaching of Christ that was laced with mercy.

The Old Testament has many foreshadows of the New Testament salvation plan and was the foundation of all that Jesus taught. The Old Testament, through the tabernacle plan, gave types and shadows of New Testament teaching which reveals a closer connection than one might see in a cursory glance. The New Testament reveals a codicil more than a different Will. The New Testament incorporates the formalities and teachings of the original testament.

Jesus said, *"These are the words which I spake unto you, while I was yet with you, that all things must be fulfilled, which were written in the law of Moses, and in the prophets, and in the psalms, concerning me."* (Luke 24:44) Paul said he *"believed all things that were written in the law and in the prophets."* (Acts 24:14)

In addition to codicil laws, there are laws to govern the incorporation of an additional document into the Will. In Florida, as in most states, an extrinsic document (not present at the time the Will was executed) may be incorporated into the Will by reference so that it is considered part of the Will. The original Will must incorporate the additional document by reference. To incorporate by reference, it must sufficiently describe the writing and it must manifest an intent to incorporate. This is a safeguard against independent documents being added later to the original Will without the intent to incorporate.

The Old Testament once again fulfills this legal requirement in the laws of God. The Old Testament makes numerous references to the Messiah that would come. More than 35 times we find His name mentioned prophetically in the Old Testament. The name YESHUA was the Hebrew name that was often translated in the Old Testament as salvation. YESHUA is the Hebrew name for Jesus, thus Jesus means salvation.

The essence of Jesus would be God and man.

"The LORD is my strength and song, and he is become my salvation:(YESHUA) he is my God, and I will prepare him an habitation; my father's God, and I will exalt him." (Exodus 15:2) *"And in that day thou shalt say, O LORD, I will praise thee: though thou wast angry with me, thine anger is turned away, and thou comfortedst me. Behold, God is my salvation; (YESHUA) I will trust, and not be afraid: for the LORD JEHOVAH is my strength and my song; he also is become my salvation. (YESHUA) Therefore with joy shall ye draw water out of the wells of salvation. (YESHUA) And in*

that day shall ye say, Praise the LORD, call upon his name, declare his doings among the people, make mention that his name is exalted." (Isaiah 12:1-4)

Isaiah foretold of His birth and the nature of His existence. *"For unto us a child is born, unto us a son is given: and the government shall be upon his shoulder: and his name shall be called Wonderful, Counsellor, The mighty God, The everlasting Father, The Prince of Peace."* (Isaiah 9:6) Isaiah said, *"A child is born"* meaning that he would be flesh and then he said *"a son is given"* meaning he would also be divinity. The essence of Jesus would be God and man.

It was foretold, Jesus would be born in Bethlehem. (Micah 5:2). It was foretold that Jesus would be a descendant of David. (Isaiah 11:1) Jesus would be a miracle worker. (Isaiah 61:1-3) Jesus would present Himself as King riding on a donkey. (Zechariah 9:9) Jesus would be betrayed by a friend for 30 pieces of silver. (Psalm 41:9; Zechariah 11:13) Jesus would be crucified. (Isaiah 53) Jesus would first present Himself as King in 173,880 days from the decree of Artaxerxes to rebuild Jerusalem. (Daniel 9:25-27) The odds are greater than 1 in 100 billion for these prophecies of Jesus to accidentally be fulfilled. I think it is safe to say that the Old Testament incorporated the message of the New Testament.

The New Testament revealed it, but the Old Testament foretold it.

One of the interesting aspects to the legality of incorporating by reference in codicil formation, is the rule that the secondary document, with some exceptions, be in existence at the time the Will was executed. It may not be present at the time the Will is executed, but it must be in existence. The Bible says that Jesus was *"the lamb slain from the foundation of the world."* (Revelation 13:8) The plan of salvation and the plan of redemption were in existence from the very beginning. The New Testament revealed it, but the Old Testament foretold it. God kept the laws of establishing an inheritance. He set the rule of Law and man copies that plan for his own laws.

CHAPTER FORTY-ONE
The Earnest of the Inheritance

❖

I was awoken early one Saturday morning by a knock on the door. The knock continued, so I gathered myself and answered the door. Two men in white apparel stood there holding a book in their hand. They handed me the book and I rubbed my eyes to focus. After a bit, I read the title: "Is the Earth running out of water?" I said, "wait just a minute." I walked to the kitchen, turned on the water, and let it run for about forty seconds. After turning the water off, I returned to the door and said, "My water supply is fine, thanks for stopping by."

The men in white apparel laughed and asked if they could come in. I cautioned them to "enter at their own risk," considering the fact that I enjoy these types of encounters more than I should. After coming into the house, they asked me if I knew Jehovah. I said that I did and that I also knew where He lived. They asked me, "Where?" I responded, "In a mobile home." They looked at me as if I had committed blasphemy. I said the Bible says, *"The Kingdom of God cometh not by observation, but that it was within you."* (Luke 17:20-21) I said, "I am mobile and so it goes where I go. If I go to school, it goes with me. If I go to the store, it goes with me. God's Spirit lives in a mobile home."

The men were getting a little restless and were ready to leave. We talked about heaven and they asked me this question as we headed to the door, "What would you do if you lived your whole life for heaven and found out that heaven did not exist after you die?" I said, "I would not feel cheated, because even if there was not a heaven to gain, and there is, this is still the best life that you could live." They left with a smile, a wave, and promised to come back. I was left with a renewed appreciation of just what the earnest of the inheritance does for us in our earthly life.

Salvation is more than just our final destination for eternity.

It never ceases to amaze me how good God is in each of our lives. He is always looking for hearts that can be touched and are willing to be changed. We may be aware of the hope and joy that God gives to humanity, but do the day-to-day blessings dull our sensitivity to the incredible miracle of salvation? Salvation is more than just our final destination for eternity.

The Bible says that we are "*sealed with the Holy Spirit which is the earnest of our inheritance*" (Ephesians 1:13-14). We understand that serving God gives us an inheritance as heirs of God. Heaven will be worth it all, but the earnest of that inheritance is what we receive now. Earnest money in a contract is the money that you give to show your interest. It is money that you put up now until the deal is closed. **The earnest of our inheritance is the part that we receive now.**

The Lord told a parable in His ministry about a prodigal son. It was a story about a rich man that had two sons. The youngest son wanted his money right away. He did not want to wait until he was older to receive his portion, he asked his father for his inheritance. His father gave it to him because he loved him, but the boy spent it all on partying and wild friends. Soon it was gone and the boy was feeding pigs. After the son returned home, the father forgave him, but the boy had spent his inheritance, and now the rest would go to his brother.

The Holy Ghost makes the adoption legal.

God gives us an inheritance, but there is a part of that inheritance that he gives us now. That is the earnest of the inheritance. He maintains the greater portion for eternity, but He gives us the Holy Spirit as a little taste of what Heaven will be like. If you enjoy the earnest, you will enjoy the inheritance. This Holy Spirit seals us. It closes the deal. The Holy Ghost makes the adoption legal.

This earnest of the inheritance does more than just bless us on a daily basis; it also keeps us focused on getting the remainder of the inheritance. The earnest of our inheritance keeps us looking at the big picture, whereas your flesh will get fixated on the present rather than on the future. Romans 8:18-19 says, "*I reckon that the sufferings of this present time are not worthy to be compared with the glory which shall be revealed in us. For the earnest expectation of the creature waiteth for the manifestation of the sons of God.*"

The earnest of our inheritance lives with an anticipation of heaven. It keeps our heart longing and looking. It keeps the sufferings of this present world in perspective. Our earnest inheritance gives us a determination to get to the destination. It also reminds us that God is not just a God of hopes and dreams; He is a God of the present.

David said, *"God is our refuge and strength, a very present help in a time of trouble."* (Psalms 46:1) David was anointed to be king of Israel. He had a bright future, but he had a lot of trouble in the present. David learned that not only can God give you a future inheritance, He can also give you a present help. An earnest on your inheritance. That's a God you want to stay close to in the present and the future.

CHAPTER FORTY-TWO
The Living Will

❖

Edwin E. (Buzz) Aldrin Jr. became one of the most famous people in the world before his 40th birthday. He and Neil Armstrong were the first humans to set foot on the moon. As Aldrin gazed across the lunar surface on July 20, 1969, he described the scene with these two words: "magnificent desolation." Little did he realize at the time that those two words would one day describe his own life as he battled alcoholism and clinical depression.

After retiring from NASA and the Air Force, the longtime military man found himself adrift with no structure in his life. Rather than feeling liberated, Aldrin was tormented by loneliness and uncertainty. "I realized that I was experiencing the melancholy of things done. I had done all that I had ever set out to do," he explained in his memoir, *Magnificent Desolation: The Long Journey Home from the Moon.*

The old fighter pilot was trapped in a death spiral of mental illness and addiction.

Too much too soon leaves us feeling empty and void.

"I moved from drinking to depression to heavier drinking to deeper depression," he writes. "I recognized the pattern, but I continually sabotaged my own efforts to do anything about it." Aldrin said he wondered whether he would have faced the same problems if he hadn't gone to the moon.

The case could be made that if one lands on the moon as a young man, what else can one do with their life to top that. How does one live the rest of life with purpose and meaning? In the world of affluence that we live in, this affects more than just old astronauts. It haunts many youth. Too much too soon leaves us feeling empty and void. Just because an individual is existing, does not mean the person is *living*. It may just be magnificent desolation.

A Living Will seems to be an oxymoron in terms. A normal Last Will and Testament comes to life at death. What is the Will suppose to do while we are living? It usually sits in an old filing cabinet deep in an attorney's office or in an attic fighting moths and moisture. It is the ultimate insurance policy. It's not really any good unless something bad happens. Perhaps, this is why we shy away from even making a Will, but this Living Will is different.

A Living Will is a document that lets the creator state his or her preferences about what type of medical treatment should be given in the event that he or she becomes terminally ill or severely injured and is unable to declare his or her intentions. A Living Will dictates whether the person is to be fed intravenously or to be put on a respirator, among other health-care directives. This document is usually prepared when a Living Trust is established. A Living Trust is a legal vehicle that is created to carry your assets during your life and to the intended destinations automatically upon your death. Thus avoiding prolonged probate procedures.

The word *living* is attached because the Living Will starts working while you are alive. It gives directions and instructions on your wishes if you are incapacitated due to medical reasons. This document is important for health care providers because they have a moral obligation to keep you alive at any cost. This document gives them permission or instruction on what to do in the difficult decisions that many families face concerning a loved one. A Living Will is intended to make the treatment or transition easier because it reflects the wishes of the patient. Whether or not it does is debatable.

The scripture says in Galatians 2:19-20, *"For I through the law am dead to the law, that I might live unto God. I am crucified with Christ: nevertheless I live; yet not I, but Christ liveth in me: and the life which I now live in the flesh I live by the faith of the Son of God, who loved me, and gave himself for me."* A Living Will may keep you alive while you are dying, but a **crucified life** will give you purpose while you are living. The real secret in life is not how to stay alive, but rather how to die.

A Living Will deals with the flesh. A dying life deals with the soul. If we focus on feeding the spiritual man, the natural man seems to follow. The opposite is not true. The Word of God is a Living

The Word of God says that if you let some things die in your life, your inner most being can begin to breathe.

Will in reverse. The Word of God says that if you let some things die in your life, your inner most being can begin to breathe. Those old desires and those old addictions in our lives should be given a proper burial so that we can come alive.

It has been said that a Living Will is a dying wish and that may be true, but the more important revelation is that a living wish is a dying will. When you and I begin to live our lives so that we can mirror the words of Christ by stating *"Not my will but thy will be done,"* we really begin to live. Until that time, the best of life is just a "magnificent desolation."

Paul said, *"I die daily."* (1 Corinthians 15:31) Paul was not enthralled with pain or suffering. He was not a masochist or infatuated with death. Paul discovered abundant life. Paul discovered that if he would die out to his will and his flesh on a daily basis, he could really begin to live. He had lived the life of climbing to the top and finding a barren land; now Paul found his calling in the chains and his destiny in the dungeons.

In the documentary, *Say Amen Somebody*, a famous man found the magnificent in the midst of the desolation when he gave this testimony:

"Back in 1932, I was 32 years old and a fairly new husband. My wife, Nettie and I were living in a little apartment on Chicago's south side. One hot August afternoon I had to go to St. Louis, where I was to be the featured soloist at a large revival meeting. I didn't want to go. Nettie was in the last month of pregnancy with our first child, but a lot of people were expecting me in St. Louis. I kissed Nettie good-bye, clattered downstairs to our Model A, and in a fresh Lake Michigan breeze, chugged out of Chicago on Route 66.

Outside the city, I discovered that in my anxiety at leaving, I had forgotten my music case. I wheeled around and headed back. I found Nettie sleeping peacefully. I hesitated by her bed; something was strongly telling me to stay. But eager to get on my way, and not wanting to disturb Nettie, I shrugged off the feeling and quietly slipped out of the room with my music. The next night, in the steaming St. Louis heat, the crowd called on me to sing again and again. When I finally sat down, a messenger boy ran up with a Western Union telegram. I ripped open the envelope. Pasted on the yellow sheet were the words: YOUR WIFE JUST DIED.

People were happily singing and clapping around me, but I could hardly keep from crying out. I rushed to a phone and called home. All I could hear on the other end was 'Nettie is dead. Nettie is dead.' When I got back, I learned that Nettie had given birth to a boy. I swung between grief and joy. Yet that same night, the baby died. I buried Nettie and our little boy together, in the same casket. Then I fell apart.

For days I closeted myself. I felt that God had done me an injustice. I didn't want to serve Him anymore or write Gospel songs. I just wanted to go back to that jazz world I once knew so well. But then, as I hunched alone in that dark apartment those first sad days, I thought back to the afternoon I went to St. Louis. Something kept telling me to stay with Nettie. Was that something God? Oh, if I had paid more attention to Him that day, I would have stayed and been with Nettie when she died. From that moment on I vowed to listen more closely to Him.

I was lost in grief. Everyone was kind to me, especially a friend, Professor Fry, who seemed to know what I needed. On the following Saturday evening he took me up to Malone's Poro College, a neighborhood music school. It was quiet; the late evening sun crept through the curtained windows. I sat down at the piano, and my hands began to browse over the keys.

Something happened to me then. I felt at peace. I felt as though I could reach out and touch God. I found myself playing a melody, once into my head. The words just seemed to fall into place:

> *'Precious Lord, take my Hand, lead me on, let me stand!*
> *I am tired, I am weak, I am worn,*
> *Through the storm, through the night lead me on to the light,*
> *Take my hand, precious Lord, lead me home.'*

The Lord gave me these words and melody, He also healed my spirit. I learned that when we are in our deepest grief, when we feel farthest from God, this is when He is closest, and when we are most open to His restoring power. And so I go on living for God willingly and joyfully, until that day comes when He will take me and gently lead me home."

-**Tommy Dorsey**
From the documentary: *Say Amen Somebody* (1983),
directed by George T. Nierenberg

CHAPTER FORTY-THREE
The Journey Beyond

❖

In 1904, a ship form the Viking Age was found and excavated in Oseberg on the west side of the Oslo Fjord, south of Oslo, Norway. The skeletal remnants of two females buried onboard were also found. Many people believe that one of the women was Queen Asa, the grandmother of Norway's first king. Furniture was found onboard the ship along with sleighs, kitchen utensils, possessions and even smaller life boats. Similar ships were found in Gokstad, Tune and Borre. These ships are on display in the Viking Ship Hall in Oslo, Norway.

I walked around the Viking Ship Museum and was amazed to learn how that many of the wealthy people in and around Norway would be buried in these ships with servants and possessions for the journey in the afterlife. They were not sure what happened after death, but they believed it would require a ship and some furniture. They were not sure what the journey beyond would entail, but they wanted to be prepared with some necessary items.

We may be carrying around a footlocker full of failure that we should unload.

This type of preparation for the afterlife is similar to what has been excavated from the pyramids in Egypt. People of wealth and means prepared for the journey beyond death by having all of their possessions buried with them. It's obvious to us now that these costly artifacts did not assist the dead. The fact of the matter is that wealth, ships, kitchen utensils and sleighs will not help us in the journey beyond. There are some necessary items, but they are not the same items that are glamorized in this life.

Mark 6:7-9 says, *"And he called unto him the twelve, and began to send them forth by two and two; and gave them power over unclean spirits; And commanded them that they should take nothing for their journey, save a staff only; no scrip, no bread, no money in their purse: But be shod with sandals; and not put on two coats."*

Unless you know what to take and what not to take, your journey will not be successful. Traveling, especially overseas, can be miserable if you take too much stuff. Most of the stuff we take on a trip is not necessary. The first thing that the Lord had to make clear to his Apostles, was what they did *not* need. He illustrated for this journey, all we need are the necessities. Some of the baggage that we are carrying in life we really do not need. We may be carrying around a footlocker full of failure that we should unload.

The tedious skill of being an attorney that composes Wills and coordinates estate planning is to know what to put in the estate and what to keep out. What is valuable and what is not necessary. The design of a Will is not to throw everything and the kitchen sink into the language of the estate, it is to know what is necessary and what is clutter. Unnecessary clutter will not only be of limited assistance it may also bog down the flow of the necessary items.

A spiritual Will is very similar. It is important to know what is necessary for the journey beyond. You must know what to focus on and what to make a part of your life. The Bible is the guide for not only this life, but the life to come. The Bible makes it very clear what is necessary for the journey beyond. The Lord said *"my yoke is easy, my burden is light."* (Matthew 11:30) This is not a process that is complicated; it is just a process of priority.

This is not a process that is complicated; it is just a process of priority.

Power

A Will must have the proper authority to be of any effect after the death of the testator. The Will has to be signed by the right parties. The correct signatures and formation gives the Will authority. It gives the Will power to function legally outside of probate. If a Will does not have authority or power, it is pushed into probate where others have to decide on what is fair and what is the intent of the testator. If possible, always avoid probate. To avoid probate we have to give the Will the power while we are alive.

The Lord did not send out His disciples empty after His death, He gave them power. The Lord said, *"Ye shall receive power after that the Holy Ghost is come upon you."* (Acts 1:8) We need the Holy Ghost, for the journey beyond. *"Except a man be born of water and [of] the Spirit, he cannot enter into the kingdom of God."* (John 3:5) *"If any man have not the Spirit of Christ he is none of his."* (Romans 8:9) *"But, if the Spirit of him that raised up Jesus from the dead dwell in you, he that raised up Christ from the dead shall also quicken your mortal bodies by his Spirit that dwelleth in you."* (Romans 8:11)

For one thousand years, all the possessions that were placed in the boats for the Vikings laid in the dirt and rotted. The dormant accumulation of wealth and possessions accomplished nothing in one thousand years. Three days after Jesus went to the tomb with power, the place was empty. Even modern space vehicles can't get out of the gravitational pull of the earth without power

In Mark 6, the disciples were told that they could take their staff as they prepared for the journey with Christ. Often in the scripture, a staff is symbolic of transformation power. The staff of Moses could turn a Red Sea into dry ground. It could turn a Nile River into a flood. It could even turn into a snake and back again. There is one thing that we can take to the grave with us. "Once I was blind, but now I see." My testimony and your testimony goes beyond this life. It is in place for the journey beyond.

Peace

One of the greatest benefits about having a Will is the peace of mind that it gives. The disciples were told to have their sandals on and be ready to go. The Children of Israel were told the same thing as they prepared to leave Egypt. Growing up in Florida, I developed a love for sandals, but what do the sandals symbolize?

Peace will walk us back to the car, after the body is buried.

Ephesians 6:13-15 says, *"Wherefore take unto you the whole armor of God, that ye may be able to withstand in the evil day, and having done all, to stand. Stand therefore, having your loins girt about with truth, and having on the breastplate of righteousness; And your feet shod with the preparation of the gospel of peace;"*

There is a peace is the mist of the storm. Peace will take us through life. Peace will take us through the hospital corridors, when we hear the news. Peace will walk us back to the car, after the body is buried.

Peace will usher us to Glory. Hear the words of Paul: *"I have fought a good fight, I have finished my course, I have kept the faith.... henceforth there is laid up for me a crown of righteousness ..."* (II Timothy 4:7-8)

There are some things that each of us will not risk being stolen. We will carry them on the plane with us. We will not check them in. We will carry it with us, because we can not risk losing it. It may be a computer or a camera, but there is one thing that is even more important when traveling to another country: Our passport. We hold it close when we are out of the country. There is a peace of mind just knowing that our passport is safe and secure on your person.

The Lord has given us a peaceport. We have the ability to move from this world to the world beyond without any trouble at the gate. When we lay our head down at night, peace covers us like a blanket. I'm not giving up. I'm not going to trade peace for a momentary pleasure. I choose peace, it is necessary for the journey. If power is our airline ticket, then peace is our passport.

If power is our airline ticket, then peace is our passport.

Praise

Mark 6 says that the disciples were not to take two coats. All the Gospels say the same thing. You could not take two. That meant that the Lord does not want us to rely on our own ability. What this means is that we could take one. He did not say do not take a coat, in fact, He expected them to take their coat. Do not take more than you need.

What is the coat? Isaiah chapter 61 says to *"put on the garment of praise."* Take praise with you for the journey beyond. Robe your life in praise. The night before the Children of Israel came out of Egypt, The Lord told Moses to tell the people; "Sleep in your robe." This instruction was given so that when the children of Israel would rise in the morning, they would be ready to go. This instruction is the same for each of us. Praise is necessary for the journey beyond.

The Egyptians were extravagant with the apparel they robed their Pharaohs in for burial. The excavation of King Tutankhamen's elaborate burial mask and gold sarcophagus in 1922 by Howard Carter in the Valley of the Kings has proven this. Even fifty clay pots that were found full of money and Tutankhamen's office seal destined to travel with the king to the afterlife. But when the Children of Israel were delivered from Egypt, the Lord told them to make sure their hand was empty. The Lord wanted them to leave Egypt with a high hand and a shout. You will need praise rather than gold for the journey beyond.

The grave can't take your praise. In the book of Revelation, the saints are gathered around the throne praising the Lord in Heaven. Some things in life we are better off to check at the gate so the burden is relieved, but then there is the carry-on bag with the important stuff that one can't afford to place in another's hands. My carry-on bag has tickets, my passport, and a coat folded up. There is usually a good book in there as well. Don't ever leave the Good Book, the Bible. It's all you need for the journey and the destination.

You will need praise rather than gold for the journey beyond.

THE FINAL VERDICT
Carry the Torch and the Tablet

❖

The journey of life has many curves and unexpected turns, but it is still the most exciting adventure afforded to mankind. The perception that life is more than just a destination motivates us to find the purpose in the prose. Living each moment with a feeling that the joy is in the journey gives us a sense of urgency to make the most of every breath. Each day has a verdict that is passed with the setting of the sun. What did we do with the opportunities that were given to us? Did we secure them or squander them?

The road map for this adventure called life is the Word of God. It not only guides us and directs us, it provides the stop signs and the street signals. The stop signs are laws. Laws that curtail our movement while ensuring our freedom and safe passage. These laws are from a loving God. The designer of humanity is uniquely positioned to know the needs of His creation. The Creator knows that excessive speed (life) and the absence of signs (laws) would not be in the best interest of His creation. If we acknowledge the supremacy of God's law and submit our lives to the same, we will understand freedom and live in freedom.

If we submit our lives to the Word of God, we will understand freedom and live in freedom.

Recently, I sat outside of a courtroom waiting for the judge to call me as a character witness for a parishioner that was attempting to put his life back together. I struck up a conversation with another man who was present for a similar purpose. He began to tell me how our nation has too many laws. The man exclaimed with conviction, if not knowledge, "We used to be a nation of freedoms and we have become a nation of laws." I tried to broaden the discussion by saying, "You know that laws are what ensures our freedoms," but my feeble attempt was lost on the emotion of the moment.

I was reminded that laws get a bad rap. Regardless of whether they are God's laws or man's laws, we still view laws as a hindrance rather than as a help. This perception of laws is only a temporary injunction; it is not the final verdict. In the end, the supremacy of God's law will shine the light of His love. The challenge for each of us is how to harness the inevitable into a *"present help in a time of need."* How can we make the most of each magical moment armed with the understanding that laws are our friends?

God used His Word to reveal His nature and our laws to reveal His love.

The Declaration of Independence attempts to ensure life, liberty and the pursuit of happiness. It was written by men that were so thirsty for freedom that they linked their liberty to the "unalienable rights" given by God. The ownership of property was fundamental to making these lofty concepts of liberty tangible. The written agreements that God gave to mankind in the two testaments, called the Holy Bible, were mirrored in our contract laws. The laws developed to make the journey realistic and enriching.

Trial law gave us a pattern to perceive how God is both our advocate and our judge. It revealed the thresholds and markers that must be met for a case to be brought against a human in the portals of Glory. The laws of evidence demonstrated how God is focused on facts. Our belief in God is more than just faith based, it is fact based. God is a giver of evidence and a judge of the lack of evidence. These laws spoke to the fact that God put a system in place that ensured enforcement and demanded deliverance based on evidence or the lack thereof.

Wills and estates uncovered how God is not temporary in nature but always looks ahead and plans for the continuance of His promises and the endurance of His gifts. Following the principle that God is both the *"Author and Finisher of our faith"* we conclude that the plan that God put in place for mankind was complete from the beginning to the end. No stone was left unturned. No detail left undone. God used His Word to reveal His nature and our laws to reveal His love.

I suppose that one cannot successfully separate the union between the laws of God, the laws of the land and the laws of our life. We are linked by the limbs that stretch pass time and distance. We will forever be connected, but make no mistake which law is supreme.

Our founding fathers described our young nation as an "experiment in democracy." This experiment survived and thrived because of the tether that our leaders fastened between the laws of God and the laws of man. Our nation has been described as a city on a hill. A city that shines the beacon of light called freedom. We built this city on hope and courage that spring from the pages of ancient scripture.

Life is freest and fullest when we take the torch of truth and run. Run with passion and purpose. Put the statue of liberty into motion. Carry the torch and the tablet. Embrace the light and the law. The verdict has already been decided, but the journey begins now.

Democracy works when those that rule are ruled by God.